Relational  Shifts ™

*A Family Doesn't Have to End
Just Because a Marriage Does.*

Julie Rappaport

Tasha Liberman

Lee Liberman

Relational Shifts Publishing
a subsidiary of Smokin Yogi Visions

Editor-in-Chief: Joy Langer

RELATIONAL SHIFTS
A Family Doesn't Have to End Just Because a Marriage Does.

Copyright © 2007 by Julie Rappaport, Tasha Liberman, Lee Liberman

For information address Smokin Yogi Visions, 8530 W 35th St, St. Louis Park, MN 55416.

Relational Shifts Web site: http://www.relationalshifts.com

Text design and layout by Sara Nurmela
Cover design by Ross Crandall

Rappaport, Julie.
Relational Shifts / Julie Rappaport — 1st ed.

ISBN 1-4196-6464-9

RELATIONAL SHIFTS

Julie Rappaport

Jessica L. Berman

Also by Julie Rappaport

The Healing of Suffering

Contents

Acknowledgments

First and foremost, and without whom this book and sister enterprises would not have come to manifestation, I must thank Joy Langer, my business partner, friend, sister-in-the-world, confident (well, mostly!) and constant support, (unless I've done something 'utterly rude' she needs to point out.) She keeps me polite and conscientious.

Joy has helped our family re-live moments that were painful, funny, poignant and insightful. Through this process, she has immersed herself in our family's life, siphoning out the book, the episodic series and a feature film! Before the book went into publication, she spent the final three months alone in her apartment, cutting, pasting and taping the morsels she found in our writings (without the help of her *rude* computer.)

She has temporarily put aside her own works to help create a company that serves those looking for positivity and potentiality in the ever-changing shifts of life. She believes in not just living or surviving, but thriving in life, which can be seen in the gestures, animation and fully engaged emotions that she uses to plunge into the heart of any matter. She is UNABASHEDLY ALIVE! I can't wait to collaborate with her to make her works come to manifestation, too.

Next, of course, I must thank Lee Liberman and, our daughter, Tasha Gittel Liberman. It is their willingness to share our family's story that allows this story to even be told. Their support, effort and excitement have continuously amazed me and I am truly fortunate and grateful to have them as my family. Lee has continuously surprised and delighted me with his 'no holds barred' kind of truths he puts out. He is still the 'Boo' to me... now, it's short for Buddha. His wisdom continues to unfold as he courageously confronts his demons and his fears.

Tasha's support, wisdom of an aged soul, and encouraging pride all have inspired me to be a better mother, daughter, niece, aunt, or other role to model for her, even if it might be modeling something she'll rebel against. We have all gone through wonderful shifts in the telling of our respective stories. Many misunderstandings have been cleared up, and many injuries mended in this very healing process. That is the point of sharing our story—to offer a platform for other families to share their own stories, and to learn from the experiences of others. I am graced, with them as my family.

My Tanta (95 year old auntie) has been one of my closest elders these last several years. She nourishes me in a sweet motherly capacity that I'm glad to bask in. Together we laugh, cry and ponder all these stories! She knows them all and still embraces all of me, even when she doesn't understand or agree with me. She is simply delighted to have my company, and her love and support have carried me through many painful moments in this process. She is waiting to see how it all turns out! What would I have done without her?

Then, there is my niece, and one of my closest friends in the world, Tammy Morgan Ratner. It was she who first said to me, "You've got to write this story down and tell it to people!" when I would read to her from my journal. Her dear friends, Samantha Vincent and Roger Mincheff, were also greatly helpful in their encouragement, introductions and advice.

My sister-cousin, Catherine Orkin Oskow, has not only been a supportive cheerleader in my journey, but has lent her excellent skills at editing to the process. Her husband, Craig Oskow, dynamically created our company logo. Their son, Kevin Ranslem Oskow, deftly created our proto-type website and other logos. In addition, my other sister-cousin, Aimee Orkin Raymond and her husband, Michael Raymond, have been greatly supportive in so many aspects that I can't even list them.

The next thanks go to Ross Crandall. Ross somehow became involved in the book production and web creation through his involvement in being the Executive Producer-and Poppa-on our demo-pilot of the episodic series, *Abnormally Normal,* that goes along with this book. The demo-pilot, *Just Breathe, Part I, She Says...* and the trailer for *Part II, He Says...* were not only a proof-of-concept for this series, but also a incredible learning experience and practice production. Ross's talent in graphic design was also put to use in our website, on our book cover and logo. Ross's belief in the projects kept him coming to the office often, and much of the time without pay. He gambled on these projects with me as a stranger. Whatever definition our relationship shifts into, I was grateful to have had him walking beside me during the journey. I know he has huge success in his future.

To Gail Rosenblum, we extend out thanks for her kind support and encouragement, and 'ink.' To Carol Mendenhall, our gratitude for speedy typing and input, as well as, Mary Carroll Moore, Deb Pflipsen, and several friends, for commentary and suggestions. Lastly, to Lynn Eang at BookSurge publishing, a division of Amazon.com, I thank her for her patience and thoroughly guiding me through publishing my **first** book. And many thanks to Sara Nurmela for spectacularly sweeping in and creating the graphic layout in one magical weekend. Whew!

Of course, there are dozens of other loved ones we thank for their support and presence in our lives.

And,

In Loving Memory of our many loved ones no longer on this earth,
We appreciate their presence and energy that have helped us get here.

May they rest in peace and their souls be vibrant.

FOREWORD

By Joy Langer, Editor

Speculations, reservations, presumptions…, call them what you will. I learned that I have tendencies towards all of them (not the representation of myself that I choose to possess.) Somehow, I had concluded for myself what this family unit must be like, even without having heard the whole story…

I had recently returned to Minneapolis after a 15 year hiatus in New York. Julie and I had a '*meant-to-be*' moment when we ran into each other… another story, but she reminded me how I had gotten my driver's license in her car, all those years ago. I laughed and said, "Remember, I was a cashier that summer at Lee's store?" Of course, she had, we were as close as sisters that year, (*funny thing, though, Lee barely remembered me*). We exchanged numbers and e-mails and looked forward to our next planned reunion, to better reacquaint ourselves. The next day she sent me an e-mail catching me up with only a few phrases, (which for Julie, I've since learned as her editor, is a major feat, in and of itself!) I clearly recall the three words that had shocked me most at first glance; Divorce, Widowed, mother--none of which she had been years earlier. Was she kidding? I thought, *if so, not funny.* She must joking; she's too young to have been through so much…*Oy, was I wrong…*

Admittedly, once hearing about all those missed years of her life, I was not only thankful and relieved that Julie was comfortable enough to discuss it, but also, that it was her life and not mine. She spoke of it *all*, with such a sense of satisfaction and relief, as opposed to what I would have imagined…I expected bitter and sad. She laughed at what I found to be the most 'uncomfortable' of places. When the word 'affair' came into play well, that's were I chimed in, "See, now *that* I'll never understand."

Julie and I both, without hesitation welcomed one another back into each others lives. Within months our previously established bond had most naturally re-booted itself. Coincidentally, I had been searching for a writing partner for quite awhile and in previous conversations we had agreed to join creative forces. With that being said, she ventured off to Hawaii, to go surf or hula or experience her first lesbian relationship *(never happened)* or whatever new explorations she was off to pursue. Before she left, I had asked, "So, where is that script you keep talking about? If we're going to do this, then now is the time." I went into the closet that she told me that it, "Must be in", found it, blew off the dust, unwrinkled its corners and found a cozy nook to read on. Within a couple of hours I called her, (knowing that she was still in route towards her tropical destination,) screaming into the phone, "Where is the rest of it?!"

AGHHH!! I felt so betrayed, how dare she entice me with these characters, then leave me with no sense of completion?! This story, even from my first quick read (*which now only feels like a remnant of what it has become,*) left me not only wanting more, but I learned something that was interesting to me, for my own self-evaluation. For the first time, I actually understood why a person might *cheat* on another. I had (from an outsider's perspective,) always ridiculed the obvious spouse, not really viewing the situation for anything other then what it seemed. No matter who the couple was, I always held judgment towards the one whom brought the third party in (*on whatever level.*) I began to have a better idea of what goes on in a marriage. It was interesting, to say the least.

This version of life's circumstances allowed me to see what one may encounter, and be forced to endure because that is what's presented and sometimes, there is no avoiding reality. It wasn't just this lesson of understanding which generated such a need to develop this piece into something more. I was also enthralled with the connections and communications between these characters (being the actress that I am,) that prompted some sort of underlining strength. That even with 'divorce' as the essence of the story, they found it within themselves to consciously make this most painful transition to transpire as painlessly as possible. *I had found our first project.*

My mother said, "What do you mean your helping to write a book about divorce? You've never even been married!" She has a point. Still, I could hardly wait for her to read it.

I explained that there was so much more to the book. There are gentle messages throughout of how relationships continually develop and change in the course of a lifetime (no matter if that relationship is that of a marriage, business or other.) There are questions presented to the reader that can be answered privately, allowing one to personalize its intention according to their own circumstances (whether the person is married, divorced or single.)

Though I've a personal relationship with Julie, Lee and Tasha, I found that it best that I separate from this reality and look at each character as the individuals that they are, but as if I didn't know them. I challenged myself to repeatedly see their unfolding as if I didn't know the outcome. I wanted the end result to be me witnessing, through their words, this family's memories, realities, feelings and overall blossoming into the 'healthful' family unit they truly are, versus my initial presumptions.

My hope is that we cultivate 'self-smarts' to become as important as 'street-smarts' or 'book-smarts.' The reason being, that I've witnessed once that inner connection happens – that knowledge of the self – honesty prevails. Communication with others from a pure place (especially in what may seem like dire times,) presents the possibility for goodness to come from those hard conversations.

I say, with confidence, that the genuineness of Julie's words resonate on every level, every pitch and every range. Lee represents himself with brutal honesty. He expresses his stories with a quick-wit, and generous detail, *at times*. Tasha bravely voices her charm and innocence with that of a child's perspective, helping to propel this 'tale' to new heights.

I am grateful to have been a part of the storytelling. This book's process of becoming an entity has been forever imbedded in me. I told my twin sister, happily married with two children in Alaska, that this will be a must-read for her book club. I assured her it would definitely generate conversation and opinions, as well as stir up dialogue amongst them that may never have been ventured into before.

Lee is ebony to Julie's ivory. Together they created a melody in Tasha. As a family, they are bringing a new song to the world.

PREFACE

First and foremost, we don't believe this is our story alone.

While the details inside are from our own marriage, the more we've talked with couples over the last decade, the more we recognize that whatever detail is the "last straw," the fact is, the symptoms of divorce are happening in at least 50% of marriages, lest we forget to mention those relationships held out of 'wed-lock'. Yet, as common as it is, a divorce, or any relationship 'break-up,' is still spoken of in hushed terms about *'what a shame.'* Divorce has been deemed 'a rampant disease in epidemic proportions that must be cured.'

What exactly is "dis-ease?" Simply put, it is the opposite of ease-- it works against nature while still being the catabolic phase of nature, itself. These days, nature is a big deal, from politics to spirituality. There are those fighting to work with and for nature against those they see as working against and abusing nature. Democracy allows the people's voices to be heard and changes to be made.

This is a story of a generation overflowing with major changes within societies, cultures, and traditions. Institutions around the world that have held power over the masses are losing control of their members, as individuals assert their rights to live as they see fit. More and more people are no longer controlled by the dogma of prescribed spirituality as their nationality, nor personality.

Moreover, this generation has more single women than not, a first in any generation in written 'his'-story. Despite those statistics, any single woman approaching 30 years old is still subject to the (good?) intentions of those reminding her that her "clock is ticking" so she'd better hurry up if she's going to have any semblance of normality in life. This continues to assert the 'spinster' versus 'bachelor' stereotypes and attach the 'good, worthwhile life' versus the 'wrong, worthless life.' However, Oprah, and millions of women alike, has defied that parable. They represent worthwhile, childless lives of single women, changing the world for the better, nurturing the children of humanity.

Yet, the business of 'courting' is bigger and broader than ever before. No longer do we have to wait for someone to come along, we can seek them out, globally, through the newest form of the 'old matchmaker,' eHarmony being just one of the many services available to find your 'true love.' In the old days, matchmaking wasn't necessarily about who might love whom, it was about what would be a beneficial partnership, not on behalf of the married souls perhaps as much as their parents. Yet there are still those who hold out for that 'chance' meeting of their 'true love' in some elevator where the world stops as the song plays…"*I'll know… when my love comes along…*" on the elevator music.

Divorce has allowed many people to un-do their 'mis-matches' and some have found their 'true love' on the 2nd or 3rd round. People are living longer, there is more time for more relationships, there is less tolerance for wasting years that melt into bitter lives. People have choices to create their lives as they wish them to be. Conversely, we all have our reasons that make up each bar of our self-designed prison we built around our lives, each rule making the space of our life a little bit smaller, limited, and giving rationality to why it is that we can not do what our heart so desires. On the other hand, the numbers of souls that are re-creating their lives during this monumental era, and the 'Relational Shifts' that the global society is experiencing, are bringing in the "End of times, and beginning of times." It is prophesized, in many cultures, that this time is at hand. *How shall we be re-born into this new life without physically dying? What transformations will we need to adapt to the new world that will present the greatest metamorphoses?*

This era of firsts, on so many levels, has affected, and effected from, the current status of marriage, family, and divorce, globally. Never before this last century, in what we call 'civilized' society, did women have the rights to possess their own property, or bodies for that fact. While more women in the world have choices, even now, we must continually debate to preserve our rights to choose, based on our own beliefs. More women than ever are consciously choosing to postpone, or even release, the ideal (or mould) of what it has meant to be a woman. With that, many have chosen to leave the 'den,' and in doing so, they have caused enough change to 'tip' the scales of normality.

Men, children, families and society, have been greatly affected by these changes: in laws, definitions, job descriptions, relationship requirements… It's hard to have integrity to both old and new thoughts— one must leave or make room for the other. History, unless re-written otherwise—will never be the same again.

In my recent History of Medicine course at the University of Minnesota, I was actually shocked to learn that male doctors invented the 'dildo' because manual stimulation of the woman took too much time. *It was a service they offered, but it bored them?* Funny, though, is the fact that many men are jealous of their woman's toys. Moreover, many insane asylums were housed with women whose sexual drives were more than the Puritanical society would accept. A woman must be *literally crazy* if she enjoys her sexuality. With sexuality as one of the bonds in a monogamous relationship, when it's missing, so is the some of the glue.

Now, looking at any magazine, movie, or otherwise publicly viewed material, women and even young girls, are made up to be sexy. "Sex sells" is the motto for several advertising campaigns. Even in getting opinions on this story which very frankly deals with sexuality, people have asked, depending on their perspective, either, *"Where are the sex scenes?"* or, *"Why is there so much about sex? Why do you have to get so personal?"*

Since we have always had a very open relationship, while trying to keep age-appropriate, I asked my wise 14-year-old daughter her thoughts, and she said, "Mom, stop worrying about what other's think. This is our story. It's nothing worse than I've seen on TV. It doesn't have too much sex, and it doesn't need anymore than it has because it's not about that."

She's right. It's not about sex; rather it's about sexuality and integrity. When our nation's biggest selling drugs 'deal' with sex drives, something is being missed in the sexuality department. Margot Anand, a leading expert in sexuality, often professes how much better off the world would be if we could forget the Puritanical impositions on our sexuality. I agree with her that it is a natural act that we, as humans, may enjoy not just for pro-creation, but also for recreation, rejuvenation, rehabilitation, and much more. Sexuality is also a door to a cosmic binding of two into one. Only birth and breastfeeding can come close to the bonding between two people. All three represent the flow of fluid and energy from one to another.

Whatever is the particular issue in the dissolution of a marriage, it doesn't matter which partner leaves, the whole family is affected by it. The fact that the marriage was already dissolving, whether all parties recognize that or not, is a direct manifestation of a universal occurrence in all phenomena, namely, change. There is a process to all things in life. They are born, manifest, and die. Only Knowledge of this natural process allows us to lighten its burdensome suffering. We can either accept this, or suffer the circumstances of life by denying its validity.

I believe, as souls, we come here to school ourselves, and do service in, of, and for the world… we come to earth in human form to learn and be schooled, as well as to teach and empower others to learn. When my stepfather died, I read a book, *Life After Life*. It changed my fledgling outlook on life and our purpose as souls on earth. It made me recognize that there was more than just this life, more outside this little world in the universe.

I had already incorporated years earlier, from the *Chronicles of Narnia*, the concept that God is seen in the capacity in which the see-er (*or seeker*) is able to *recognize divinity*. Recognition comes from repeated experiences we learn as children, not only from our family, but from our cultural society at large. If, and when, we have an experience of God that is outside of what we have learned God to be, than confusion and loss of faith follow. Viktor Frankl writes, in his book *Man's Search for Meaning*, about living in concentration and death camps. He theorizes about how people were able to cope under such dire situations and what motivated them to survive the abhorrent circumstances. Did they continue to live by will alone, or did they succumb to being victims? What force was underneath their will to survive? Anger? Perhaps, for some. Nobility and fear battled each day in the war room of their minds. What was the right thing to do, care for oneself and survive, or care for others and perish sooner? Some lost all faith and became only for themselves, while others continued to shine as a light for those who would not lose faith. Many, who did survive, cared for others and in doing so, cared for themselves. Frankl blended science with humanism, and shared his belief that humans' primary motivational force to survive is their search for meaning.

Fear rides on hope. Meaning rides on purpose. Having faith complements truly knowing there is a purpose to our lives beyond what we can fathom, and allows us to use our lives to find meaning and purpose.

It seems to me, though, that the world today is teetering between blind faith and lost faith. There is reasonable faith in between these two fear-based views. When blind, we cannot possibly see the truths that are right in front of us. When lost, we can not recognize signs along the way that guide us. When centered in clarity, we can balance our actions with wisdom. Clarity comes from knowing what is right, and doing it, even if others believe you are wrong. When your own clarity is based upon intentions of the highest good for all concerned, you needn't worry about which path is right or wrong, your body and conscience will tell you loud and clear, if you will listen.

But our minds cloud our truths with second-guessing fears. Literally. The amalgam is the center of 'fear' in the brain. Under a newer type of image resonation, called a PET scan, the color red covers the area of the amalgam while the frontal lobes are in other colors, depending on the level of conscious activity. When a Vietnam Vet underwent a PET scan during a Post Traumatic Stress flashback, the red color of the scan covered all the way over the frontal lobe. This is evidence for our inability to think clearly, when we are filled with fear. We make rash decisions when based on fear. *We have nothing to fear, but fear, itself.*

I believe in reincarnation and that each time we return to life, we are working towards completing a level while entering yet another. Sometimes, we have to work especially hard in one particular area that comes up again and again until we are able to understand its lessons and move on to the next level, having finally acquired the appropriate background and understanding to succeed as we continue our education. You cannot study quantum physics without understanding the basic concepts of calculus. *Or, can you?*

I've never been a linear learner or 'do-er', for that matter. It's something that has caused… frustration, for me as well as others whom have worked or lived with me. If they are linear, I seem to be a random chaotic wind that blows their neat habits into a mess, in which they don't work so well. Even still, while I haven't taken the 'correct' paths to learn about quantum physics, my studies (from the plethora of interests that call my name each day) have somehow prepared my mind to think in terms of quantum physics, even though I may not yet be able to articulate scientific rhetoric about it. The concepts are there, swimming in my mind and through my veins. It is, perhaps, my next level of education. These last few years, aside from finishing my undergraduate degree finally, have been geared towards synthesizing the lessons of my life (many wrapped up in this nice little package.)

In our life lessons, it is not that we can ask for strength, and then, *zap,* we're strong. No, the lessons deal with providing you opportunities to strengthen yourself. How many broken ribs does it take to become a black belt, or falls to make that triple-axel spin? Or any other type of champion? What are the circumstances that allow us to build our strength? We are not given strength, but opportunity to build it. Only we can choose to use it. Each time we fall, or are even pushed down, we choose to get back up and try again, or we give up. We can blame others, but it is our decision. It is our own life and we can give its power away, or we can take it back and learn to use it wisely.

The next joke the universe plays on us, in the karmic cycle of educational lives, is when we ignorantly say, "Oh, I get it! And that person over there does not!" My interpretation is that the universe says back, "Really? Let's see how well you 'get it' and that person does not." We, then, have yet another opportunity to witness ourselves during these 'exams.' Whether or not we choose to use them as lessons for ourselves, rather than trying to force them on others, is the next pop quiz.

This recognition has made me quite aware of the words I use, and even my thoughts. The thoughts still come, as the practice of weeding a garden never ends, nor does the practice of weeding my un-positive thoughts.

I've finally found myself a 'life coach' to help me weed the toxins and prepare the soil of my new garden of my life. She taught me about death for the reason that I would learn to enjoy and savor life. She teaches me about Karma and my soul's journey. She teaches me I can only change how I react to anything, but I cannot change the circumstance, or the very nature of life itself. She is my guide, my conscience, my confidant, nemesis, prompter, and my bright shining light. She glows even if the light at times is dim. She manages to find the one place to peer a ray through my darkness. She's unexplainable, and yet everything familiar. She is me. I am grateful for her, for me.

Gratitude means more than money, goes farther, lasts longer, and never empties. I am grateful for my family and friends and even my nemeses, too. Through them, my life lessons and the opportunities to expand my awareness vibrate at a higher frequency, and resonate the goodness I can consciously cultivate.

We offer our story to you, dear reader, in an effort to open minds, dialogues and hearts to your own stories, or the stories of those you love. Looking at life as a bigger picture than our daily disturbances (road rage, or someone taking advantage of us…,) we can recognize each bout of depression, elation, defiance or compliance, as only one aspect of the human nature that we are here to learn. In learning this, we grow our compassion for others, as well as ourselves. In growing our compassion, we weed a bit more of the bitterness that is so easy to succumb under its pressures. In weeding our bitterness, we can recognize that our relationships are the soil in which we grow our selves and nourish that with which we come in contact. Relationships are a result of our garden, as much as they shape our garden, or tapestry, or song… however, you like to make the analogy.

What we grow, we give to our children to feed and fuel their growth. We want them to be cautious, not to make the same mistakes we made. But then we must share with them of our mistakes, rather than hide them, if our children are to believe we can understand how they've made their own. And, they will continue to make their own 'mistakes' in order to learn their own lessons, like mistaking infatuation with an idea for real love.

One of my favorite little books (the kind that fit in your purse,) is called *Try Again, Fail Again, Fail Better…* It's filled with little antidotes about people who have experienced major successes in life, but only after allowing themselves to make major mistakes, and then keep going after evaluating what happened. They learned from and incorporated those 'failures' into their next level of revelation. It has quotes from Benjamin Franklin, Henry Ford, and here two of my favorites, both from Winston Churchill:

Success is the ability to go from one failure to another with no loss of enthusiasm.
(Who hasn't expressed loss of enthusiasm for love after a painful loss?)

...Never—in nothing, great or small, large or petty—never give in except to convictions of honor and good sense... Never give up.

For Lee and me, we never gave up on the honorable conviction that made good sense...

A Family Doesn't Have to End Just Because a Marriage Does!

Did we use good sense through all of it? Of course not! However, we learned a great deal from all our "mistakes." If we are able to save any marriages through our book, then we are very blessed. But if we are able to save any families through our stories, than we have succeeded, despite our failures, and are blessed and grateful to have lived them.

We share our story with you.

PROLOGUE

Dreaming the Voyage of Life

Lee: When I got married, I never thought that I would get divorced.

Julie: *When I got married, I thought I was going to do it better than I had witnessed. I thought I knew the potential problems. I desperately wanted to believe that we would be able to work through them because our love for one another was so true. We were soul mates. For some reason, I also thought through marriage, I would finally be considered an adult, having always been the "baby" of the family.*

Lee: When I got divorced, I never thought it would be like this.

Julie: *When I got divorced, I knew I did not want to be hateful or bitter, even though it would have been easier to go into blame and shame. I knew I wanted to teach my daughter to love herself and her life. I knew I would have to learn to model that.*

Lee: When I found out my wife wanted out of our marriage, my feelings of losing her were so great that I did not think that I could live without her. She used to tell me that I didn't love '*being married to her,*' but rather I loved the '*idea of being married*' and it happened to be her. At the time, I could not really understand this, but after Julie told me she wanted a divorce, I began to see what she was saying.

Julie: *When I finally gave him the letter asking for a divorce, I was so scared, and yet so sure, of what I was doing. We had talked about getting divorced for almost our whole marriage! How we would do it, what we wouldn't do… Whether it was our friendship, our money, our daughter, our friends, our possessions… we had discussed it on so many levels. I guess he never thought it was a serious conversation. He was humoring me, saying what I wanted to hear. Just talking about how holier we would be than the others we had witnessed. I have to admit, as much as I loved him, it felt like I unlocked the self-designed prison I had made for myself. The real me was getting out and I was excited about my life. The only problem was that I was hurting him and Tasha in the process…It was like a necessary surgery that had been avoided too long. Pain, but anticipation of healing.*

Lee: I was brought up to think that marriage is what we, as humans need to be fulfilled. I was a person that needed someone living with me. I needed someone to come home to. I needed that security blanket to be next to me, behind, or in front of me.

Julie: *I was brought up to think that I could do anything I put my mind or body to. Actually, I also heard my mother say, "I'm nothing without a man in my life!" This powerful woman, who could do anything, was implying it was all a farce. Without a man, it's not worth anything for a woman to be alone. I thought I was going to make my first million dollars before I'd allow myself to marry. On the other hand, Lee was so persuasive, and marriage seemed such an easy way to get out from under my mother's rules. If married, I'd make my own house rules.*

Lee: Redefining divorce was not a concept I understood. Moreover, I know many people are in that same position, which is why I'm writing this book—to help people who are going through divorce make it a more conscious proactive process, rather than just reactive. Besides, this book is not just for the husband, wife and children, but also for the people that are surrounding the family that is experiencing the divorce, or "Relational Shift," along with them.

Julie: *Redefining Divorce was a concept that came from my own rebellious behavior, I guess. I don't believe we have to live in a box. If you look at the box as if it sat upon the world, however big or small, and moved outside that box, you just put yourself inside the opposite box on the sphere. Definitions create boxes around concepts or relationships that explain them. "Check the box" for your marital status, age, gender... The boxed concept around divorce is that it is an unhealthy reaction to a problem. I want to live without a box, to explore and utilize what is either in or outside of that imaginary box.*

Either the product of marriage is fishy or over half of the population are unable to grasp the spirit of marriage. If a consumer group were evaluating it, I would say the concept would flunk, just looking at the numbers. Yet, there are dozens of wedding magazines, and barely a few magazines that dare to touch upon the real lives of married or divorced families.

Lee: I'm very comfortable with our relationship now. I feel great when we are together or when we talk on the phone. There isn't a thing we can't say to each other—not like in our marriage where we were always walking on eggshells. We are best friends, soul mates for life. However, many do not understand us. They think something else is going on.

Julie: *Now, my relationship with Lee is so much more enjoyable and healthy. We laugh a lot together now, as we used to. We still fight, plenty. However, our relationship has always had a brother-sister quality. We fight. Okay, next.*

Even now, there are still days of walking on eggshells, but their duration is much shorter—minutes compared to months. We've both lost much in our lives, and gained much too. I am happy to talk with him every day. We even still have family nights, go on family vacations, and enjoy spending time with each other's families. We're still aunt and uncle to all our wonderful nieces and nephews. No one worries about having us in the same room.

I guess I think there are some things we avoid talking about. When we do discuss those hard subjects, even when fighting about them, we know the other is a dear person with whom we disagree on certain things. Maybe a stubborn person-but a dear person.

Lee: Why did we get divorced if we spend so much time together? How did we develop such a great relationship—one that not only benefits our daughter, but also us—through our decision to divorce?

Julie: *How can you divorce your best friend? How can a better family be created through divorce, or "Relational Shifts?"*

Lee: These are just a few of the many questions this book will answer, and provoke.

CHAPTER ONE

Blueprints Drafted

Julie

With his thick Israeli accent booming just a little too loud over the hushed audience, Lee's father points to me, a high school senior, up on stage, playing Maria in our synagogue's youth group production of *West Side Story*.

"Now, why can't you go and find a girl like that? That's the kind of girl you marry!" he said to Lee. *Little did he know.*

My stepfather, whom I adored and adored me, had just passed away earlier that week. I didn't know if I could do the performances. At the end of the first night's performance, as *Maria* holds the gun, pointing it wildly and then at herself, my true emotions were able to explode out from me in front of the knowing audience.

One year later, Lee's first cousin, who was my best friend and roommate at that time, set us up on a blind date. She told me that it had always been a family joke that he would marry the daughter of family friends. Instead, the daughter ended up falling in love with Lee's older brother and marrying him. During their (2ⁿᵈ) ritual wedding ceremony in Israel, Lee started dating her younger sister. He returned home, but quickly went back to Israel with an engagement ring. The sister had no intentions of marriage.

I met him one month later, back here in Minnesota. *Wouldn't he be on the rebound, though?* I wondered.

His cousin happened to be mad at both of us for some reason at that time. None of us, all still friends these decades later, can remember why she was upset with us, but we all recall she thought setting us up on a blind date was a perfectly hysterical way to get back at us for whatever grievances she had with us. She thought we would hate each other because we were so different: Lee was a right-wing introvert, and I was a left-wing extrovert. He cared about cars, jewelry, and looking right. I cared about people, places, and feeling right.

Lee and I had met a couple years earlier. When I first saw him, he didn't make such a great impression. I was good friends with his younger sister. The day she introduced us, he barely looked up from the TV, much less said hello.

I thought, *"Ohhhh, aren't we special!"* He was older by four years. We were simply high school girls, not worth a glance.

Lee and I had a very special connection right from our first date, though. He picked me up from his cousin's house, where I was living at the time. Her family was watching from the windows. It was exciting and irritating at the same time. Nice, after my mother's rejection, that a family was involved in my life, yet irritating that they were inspecting our every move.

On our first date, Lee picked me up in his new car, a Datsun 280 ZX. He was so proud. I was not much into cars or men that were preoccupied with them, but I tried to be interested and polite. It's how I was raised. If you want someone to like you, treat them nicely. *Why I felt this way is a whole other chapter, or book…*

We went to the Nankin, a Chinese restaurant that was a Jewish hangout back then. We had Wanderer's Punch served in large laughing Buddha mugs and talked for four hours! He wanted to know my whole life story. Never short on words, I told him. He asked for it…

> *My stepfather had died the year before--my senior year in high school—on the exact date my biological father had died fourteen years earlier. It was the week I starred in the play where Lee first saw me (not including the brief introduction from his sister a couple years earlier.)*
>
> *My long-time high school boyfriend found it difficult to support me during this very rough period in my life. We broke up. I felt miserable. My family spread apart after my stepfather's death, the similarity to our real father's death being too hard to endure once again. I really had no one to talk to about how I felt about myself, or about the dreams I lost when he died.*
>
> *Our family may have looked like the Jewish version of the Kennedy's from the outside; we were more like the Ford's. We were in that ring of society that upheld our family on a pedestal. Behind closed doors, though, there was a pervading illness. My mother's physicians continued to prescribe her the latest Valium or Halcion or Seconal--whatever was new on the market. He was a doctor, after all, and we should always listen to what they tell us. Addictions occurred with each doctor prescribing more meds for my mom (in the Valium-happy 1960's and more advanced drugs in the 1970's) after my father's death--to help her cope with the loss on top of raising five children. She needed sleep. They helped her. She was exhausted by the time she had to deal with my own*

travails, especially with my young adulthood coinciding with her grief, and the stigma of a second widowhood...

In my misery, I started sleeping with--well, it seemed like everyone (including the pool boy.) To this day, I still shudder at the memory of one boy's whining, "Come on, you've done it with everyone else...can't you just let me do it, too?" The lowest point of my life was getting out of that boy's bed. I wanted to vomit all over myself, spew all of myself out of me until there was nothing left of this pathetic shard of this girl I had become since my stepfather died.

When my mother sifted through my diary and found out what I was doing, rather than realize how deeply I needed help and guidance, she threw me out of the house. (What would the pool boy think of **her***?!) It was always what others would think about her when they saw me. I was a mess, a messy reflection of her. (Sometimes, it's hard to look in the mirror.)*

My oldest sister lived in California with her husband and children. I moved out there for college, to be near someone in my family that loved me even though I was such a wreck. She was helpful and supportive, but she also had her own life and family and could only do so much.

When I got to California, I thought I could re-create myself. No one knew me. I could earn my self-respect back, and start fresh. But, you know the saying,...

"Wherever you go, there you are."

I fell in love with a man ten years older, a graduate student at the school. He was a true gypsy: a dancer, a juggler, and a wonderful lover. He taught me how to eat fire! We had a wonderful short romance. My new love said he would follow me to Minneapolis, convert to Judaism and marry me. My family was humored by it. There she goes again....

I knew before the year was over that I needed to return to Minneapolis and try to repair the damage I had caused, to try to make amends with my mother while still being good to myself.

But, how?

I had never believed in therapy, but I went to a therapist through my college to help me make a plan for when I went back home. I felt I was an independent woman of the Eighties, but I still needed some guidance from a healthy being, male or female.

This therapist and I agreed that living in my mother's home would be detrimental to repairing our relationship. My mother did not agree, and refused to acknowledge that—with the little tools I had—I was doing the best I could to try to become a family again, one where we could count on each other, through thick and thin.

I wanted my family to have a "Happily Ever After" even behind closed doors, however, it was just not meant to be. The situation between my mother and myself continued to disintegrate.

Upon hearing my life's highlights and low points, Lee wanted to save me from my life's troubles there and then. I told him not to put me on a pedestal. I had much to learn in life. It fell on deaf ears. He said I was the "real thing."

Then, he took me home, told me what a spectacular time he had-and left!

No kiss. No nothing. This was a first in many years!

I was shocked. I thought we had had a great time together. Why wouldn't he kiss me goodnight? Much less not want to have sex. *Wow, I* thought, *this guy must really respect me. Knowing I've felt so used by men, he didn't want to put me in that position.*

He was so nice and sweet. He sent me a bouquet of roses the next day. WOW! But, I was such a wildcat at that point in my life that I almost invited in the cute delivery boy, until I found out he was Lee's best friend. *Tacky, tacky.* I suppressed the urge.

We went on a second date. When he brought me home, instead of kissing me goodnight, he stood at the door and told me, "I don't want to get hurt, but I know that you are the one for me. Am I the one for you?"

I didn't know what to say but the truth. I was flattered, but it was a little scary, all the same. It was as if it wasn't about me, he just needed to get married. *RUN!* Right?

When I think about it now, I can recognize the phrase, "Looking for love in all the wrong places." I thought at the time, that I wasn't looking to get married, but in truth, every man I dated was somehow a potential husband!

I think a lot of women my age can relate to what I was going through in what was still my late adolescence. We had the pill and no one had heard of AIDS. We were the generation after the sexual revolution, and STD's just weren't prevalent. Somehow, I thought that sex equaled love, and that it might fill the void of loss permeating me.

To answer Lee's daring question, I explained I was only eighteen, and dating several people I enjoyed, and that after only two dates, I couldn't possibly answer a question like that, no matter how great he was or how comfortable I felt around him. I didn't even know how he kissed or what his birth date and astrological chart were... *I'd have to consult the stars, first.* He told me his birthday and I almost fainted. I promptly told him I would not be able to see him any longer. *"WHY?!"* He couldn't understand what I was talking about. I believed it was a sign. It was the same birth date as my real father's, and damned if I was going to repeat my mother's existence, and end up widowed!

Lee laughed at this and said he understood, but that he would continue to try to convince me. And convince me he did. *Just why am I so convincible...?*

While driving somewhere on our fifth date, he finally asked if he could kiss me. I told him I was surprised it had taken him so long to ask! He pulled over, made a big flourish of parking, then looked me straight in the eyes as he gently kissed me on the lips for only a split second. He pulled back, gave a huge sigh, and continued driving with a look of full satisfaction on his face. I didn't know what to do with this. All I could think of was that he respected me too much. He must not have wanted to put himself into the position of not wanting to stop. *Right?*

He courted me with a style that was right out of the movies. He set up walks through Wirth Park with a bottle of wine and a picnic. He bought me jewelry (before he realized jewelry was not my thing--I was an insurance hazard, losing one piece after another.) He took me on a two-week driving trip across the country in his sport hotrod of a car. After several fights, he finally allowed me to drive it.

We went to fancy dinners, on boat rides at his family's cabin, and had Shabbat dinners with his Israeli family every week. They had so much fun together, even if all that Hebrew was overwhelming. The women all cooked together while the men sat and smoked. I was always more comfortable with the men, and since I was a guest, it was acceptable that I sit and not work.

Such a gentleman, such a family...such potential. I had never been so courted and it was thrilling and surrealistic at the same time. What exactly was I signing up for here?

I started following his horoscope, too.

Lee and I continued dating openly. *I don't know who else he was seeing, but I was totally honest with him.*

One time there was an accidental overlap when another man I was seeing showed up unannounced at my mother's house while I was there with Lee. Lee was a total gentleman about it, acknowledging that it was an embarrassing situation for me, and making the best of it. The uninvited man, on the other hand, was as rude as I have ever experienced someone to be. Lee tried to make conversation, asking him about his work, and I remember his actual response was, "It's too complicated to explain to you, you wouldn't understand it, so I won't even bother."

I was appalled.

I had witnessed how they each treated their own mothers. Lee was respectful, helpful, adoring and affectionate with his mother. The other fellow treated his mother disdainfully, bossing her around or complaining about her performance. I had heard, "If you want to know what a man will treat you like, watch how he treats his mother." The message came through loud and clear. Lee seemed to present a future relationship that was kinder than this man probably ever could offer.

Meanwhile, my college love kept calling me from California. I thought we were making plans for him to move to Minnesota. I told Lee about these plans. He suggested I stop moving forward with this relationship. My oldest brother agreed, saying, "You're going to marry a juggler?" If I pursued this love, would I be living in this man's horse trailer on the campus parking lot?

I was accustomed to quite a higher lifestyle. I didn't really consider myself a 'country club girl,' but in reality, I was. This started to haunt me, as well as the fact that my family had already said that they would not approve of this man. People may have thought I was such a rebel, but I wanted security as much as the next person. I had seen enough to know—I had lived quite a sheltered life. How would I support myself?

Plus, Lee's courtship and tender caring were helping me fall in love with him. We finally began to have a sexual relationship. Sometimes, he could make my knees melt just by kissing me, *sometimes*. Although he had been sexual many times before our relationship—his understanding of sexuality was lacking. Once, halfway (or so I thought) through making love, Lee got up and walked away. I asked him where he was going. He said he was finished and was going to clean up. I told him that I wasn't finished and invited him back. He laughed, saying, "Oh, really? Like you're going to have an orgasm or something?!"

I was shocked. Was he pulling my leg? My over-experience with men made me realize that he wasn't kidding. We had a long discussion. I tried to convince him that women really did have orgasms and enjoyed sex. It wasn't just about lying there like a dead fish and getting their man off. He didn't believe me. He tried humoring me, saying he'd think about it. I wanted to believe that he would think about it seriously, and learn about women's sexuality. Why wouldn't he?! Apparently, he had never been taught about the sexual part of a loving relationship.

The subject came up… many times. He kept asking me to marry him, and I kept trying to tell him that a good sex life was an essential glue, aiding a good marriage in holding together through turbulence and calm. I worried that I knew too much for my own good about sexuality, but I wanted to share it with him in a way that allowed us to have that important part of a marital relationship.

Looking back, I now see how desperately I wanted to be part of a family again. Maybe Lee was the way to recreate what I had lost. After all, his family adored me. I would be their first natural born American in the family. They practically courted me too! They would frequently talk about us getting married and what could they do to help me make up my mind. We hung out with them all time. The family-ness of it was intoxicating. They treated me so well, were always thrilled to see me, and wondering what was going on in my life. And, when would I finally marry Lee!?

Maybe having a great sex life isn't what a good marriage is about, I thought. Maybe, that's all mumbo-jumbo-psycho-babble. Maybe being part of a family was what life was about, and maybe mature sex was about procreation and not just for fun…

I needed some guidance. Lee seemed to be the only one to have my best interests in sight. He was looking out for me, but he did have his own interests in there, too.

I had many conversations with Lee about how strongly he wanted to marry me because his family wanted him to marry me. He finally admitted that was true, but also declared his love for me was real. I wanted to believe it. I loved him very much. I saw we had such potential.

I remember one night, after four months of intensive courting, he asked me to marry him for maybe the twelfth time. Even though we had fought on our recent vacation together, and our sex life hadn't gotten much better as he had promised it would, I was so in need of being loved and cared for, that I lightly answered, "If you have the guts to ask my mother for my hand, then I'll marry you!"

Later that week, Lee showed up at my mother's home, doused in a bottle of expensive cologne, and dressed so debonair. My mother, who normally would never be caught 'undone' and came from a line of 'best dressers,' entered the room in her schmata robe, blue face-mask and hair curlers under a plastic shower bag for this ceremonious meeting. Did she do that on purpose just to scare him off?

She spent two hours telling us why she would not allow her eighteen-year-old daughter to get married. Wasn't sinking in. Lee finally cut her off. "We'd like your blessing," he said, "But, we are going ahead with it, either way!"

I was so impressed that he stood up to her. I knew I finally had someone in my court again. No one had stood up for me to my mother since my stepfather had passed away.

We left the house, giddy with conquest. I was so proud of him, and for me. That was scary! I didn't think we'd make it out of there. Lee was victorious.

As we were driving, the whole sky undulated with meshing and weaving ribbons of color, and a primordial sound echoed and vibrated to the very core of my being. Every hair on my body was standing on end. I felt as though all was right in the universe.

I made Lee pull the car over so we could watch the lights. Was it some Sound & Light show nearby? We were late to meet his friends and he wanted to go—something I would learn over the years, being late was not acceptable, no matter what the universe laid out for us to contemplate.

Later, when I found out it was the Northern Lights, I knew there was some cosmic significance. Lee and I had made the right choice to be together. The heavens choreographed a performance in our honor!

I never saw Northern Lights like that again. *Lee and I still joke about it-- that he still owes me a trip to Norway to see them… Maybe our next family trip?*

Yes, there were already red flags of our future problems. Yet, he was attempting to become part of my life, as well as inviting me into his own. My life was bordering absurd compared to what Lee had been exposed to in his life. He was a party-guy, hung out with the blonde crowd and his idea of culture was sports. Mostly wrestling. He LOVED wrestling. I mean the World Wide Wrestling TV shows and magazines… The game he and his buddy made up--well, we could have been gazillionaires in that cult society. I *tried* having fun, front row seats and all.

I, on the other hand, hung out with the theater and dance crowd. I had only been to one sport event in my life, and was bored to death. The theater crowd is very on the edge of society, it pushes the envelope. Lee didn't really get there was an envelope, until he met me. Poor guy. During our courtship, he even came to a theater-crowd costume party, dressed in drag, just to do my bidding. His friends heard about his outfit and said he was 'whipped.' I think he had a mission and was willing to do whatever it took. His get-up was hysterical, but a valiant effort that I could not dismiss.

He was really trying to open his mind to new things. With that, we could soar together.

I called the country club where I had grown up and would have my "to-die-for" wedding the following month. I wanted to find out about the "Junior" Membership, for the married kids of members who haven't financially established themselves yet, and were under 25. I had all the qualifications, I thought. It seemed I was missing the piece in my pants that my privileged brothers, but neither myself or my sisters, possessed. "Oh, honey, junior memberships are only for the sons."

It was the first time I truly experienced sexual discrimination. It was 1983! Were 'the clubbers' left so far behind modern society or did I just not understand the inequities of 'equal opportunity'? I responded, "Wow! Are you serious? I bet the news and the state courts would have a ball with this!"

It took only ten minutes for a return phone call. I was told I had changed the board policy, daughters would now be admitted as junior members, as well. I felt like I just had my first major victory in undoing injustice in the world. It worked to open my mouth and say something was unfair. Not really in my family circle, but outside of it, I had found a strong voice that had potential to change the world for the better. The problem: the club told me the price of the junior membership. After choking and admitting we couldn't afford that, we didn't join the club, after all.

My family thought Lee and I should live together before we made such a huge decision. I was only nineteen. What did they know of my wants and needs and dreams? Nothing, it felt. So, I chose to believe in Lee and his family, in what they offered in support and love.

We were going to sail through life's problems together, undeterred, a force to be reckoned with if you got in our way.

Lee - 1

Julie Rappaport played the lead, Maria. I remember the first time she came on stage. Wow. I thought, what a gorgeous girl! I had always gone out with non-Jewish girls, a decision not very well accepted in my family. The minute I saw Julie, something hit me. My dad thought she was special, too, and asked why I couldn't date a nice girl like that. Me being the shy guy, I never made a move after that night.

When I look at the reasons of why I thought I wanted to get married, I would have to say because it was the right thing to do at that point. My parents instilled in me, along with friends and relatives, that my life would have no meaning without being married and raising a family. At that time, I was not really able to think for myself, but I was looking to please my family and to become the kind of person that they wanted me to be, and society would accept. *I was not looking for a mate. I was hunting for one.*

My older brother had just married the woman who—the entire time we were growing up--I thought I was supposed to marry. She was a close friend of the family. Her family was still in Israel, where my family originated. Our parents always joked that when we grew up, we would be married. I used to take it for granted this was true. I never really tried to understand love, or what it meant.

It was kind of like a set-up marriage, and it suited me just fine. After all, what was marriage about? All I knew was that marriage was about two people committing to each other to marry, raise kids, work hard and grow old together.

During my brother's wedding, of course, everyone kept saying that I was next. When would I find someone to marry and start a family? The pressure was on. I fell in love with the bride's sister. Wow, fell in love. Yeah, right. I picked the next easiest thing. How natural that two brothers should marry two sisters with whom their parents' were best friends. *What would my sister do, since they had no brother?* Crazy as it may seem, this is what was running through my mind during all this time. I started dating her sister with the intentions of marriage, but this was not on her mind. Broke my heart again? No. Just had to move on and find someone else to marry.

Now, along came Julie, perfect in every sense. Different from anyone I had ever met, or was told was even out there. Julie was free, alive, adventurous, willing to take chances and not be controlled by thoughts of others. She was able to speak her mind. The first time I saw Julie was at my parents' house a few years earlier. I was a cool teenager, not very interested in my younger sister's friends. I remember coming home, running upstairs, saying a quick hello, but not really looking at her.

The next time our paths crossed was at a youth play at our family's synagogue. My sister had a bit part in *West Side Story* and I was forced to go see her. That's when I really first saw Julie.

It wasn't until a year later, fate would have it that my cousin asked me if I wanted to go on a date with one of her best friends. This friend was staying with my cousin because she wasn't getting along with her mom. I asked her who it was, and she told me it was Julie Rappaport. I remembered her name from the play. I was very excited, but too cool to let my cousin notice it. To be safe, I asked her if I could see a picture. Sure enough, it was Jules. I told my cousin to *set it up.*

I remember getting ready to pick up Julie. I wanted to make a good impression. I made sure that my car was washed and polished to the point where I could see my reflection in it. I must have tried on ten different outfits, put on five different colognes, and brushed my hair a hundred times. At that time, Porsche glasses were very in and I had a pair. I had my shirt open so that she could see what hair I had on my chest. Look today at *That 70's Show* and you will see my outfit. Even if it was 1982.

I checked my reflection and straightened my hair before I went to ring the doorbell. Julie was not ready yet, as I would soon become accustomed. Finally, Jules came upstairs. Lord have mercy, I thought. She was beautiful. Her face was a painting of a goddess. I wanted to spend some time with her, show off to her, and make her like me. I took her to one of the best Chinese restaurants in Minneapolis.

At dinner, we talked for hours. I felt we connected on a level that I have never connected with any other woman. I wanted to be with her forever. I knew that we belonged in each other's lives somehow. I took her back and walked her to the door. I wanted her to think that I was a gentleman.

The next day, I called my best friend and asked him to go pick up some roses from the florist and deliver them to Jules from me.

I was working for my dad and could not leave my job. When he delivered them, Jules opened the front door wrapped in a towel; she had just come out of the shower. My best friend in the whole world almost gave her those flowers from himself.

I really didn't know how to act around someone I deeply cared about. I was always too worried about how she might perceive me. I hoped that the way to be around her would just come to me naturally. Magazines, books and TV were where I got most of my information on how to act with women—and in Julie's case, it wasn't nearly enough. I didn't want her to think I was just after sex.

One beautiful autumn afternoon, I picked up Julie and we went to Theodore Wirth Park. We walked down a path and reached an old cabin just as it started to rain. I had brought a bottle of wine. We stayed for quite a while. She mesmerized me. I had never met a person like her. She was smart, worldly, opinionated, and extremely beautiful. I loved talking to her. She could talk about all subjects, except sports. That didn't bother me much because I was so much into her that I forgot about all sports, except wrestling.

Although my mind said immediately, and I remember telling her as well, that I didn't want to be hurt again, meaning that *if you do not want our relationship to end up in marriage, let me know now.* I wanted to marry her. I thought I had fallen in love with Julie, but at that time, I had no real idea of what love was about or what marriage meant. Before we were engaged, we took a driving trip together to the West Coast and back to Minnesota. How cool at that age to take a driving trip in a black, two-seater sports car with a gorgeous woman by my side. I also thought it would be a great way for just the two of us to be alone for two weeks and see how, and if, we would get along, being with each other 24 hours a day. My folks, of course, had no problem with it--anything to help get Julie and me closer. On the other hand, Julie's mother had a major problem with it. "What will everyone in the community say?"

I told her we didn't really care what people said. We wanted to go and we were going. I knew that she thought I was a good person, responsible, came from a good family, a respected family, but I am sure that she wasn't expecting me to take her daughter on a two-week vacation when we weren't married. Maybe that was something she would expect from Julie, but not from me.

My parents let Julie sleep over in my room the night before

we left on this trip. I don't quite remember if we made love that night, but as I look back now, it seems my parents really wanted me to make it with Julie.

In high school, I always dated non-Jewish girls. It seemed to me that the Jewish girls were not really the kind of girls I was interested in dating. I wanted a person to be able to sit down with and communicate about life's adventures, or just hang out with and be friends. Most of the Jewish girls I met in high school were about looks and being at the right place with the right people. Many just wanted a boyfriend so they could go out as couples. If you weren't hooked up, you weren't part of the scene. The *goyim*, as my father called the non-Jewish girls, liked to party, go to football games, hang out alone or in crowds...those kinds of girls just attracted me more.

My parents never liked the girls I dated. If I ever brought home a girl who wasn't Jewish, my dad would make it a point not to meet her and sometimes would snub them when I introduced him to her. *Pretty much rude.* I respect him for keeping to his beliefs that Jews should date or marry Jews to keep our culture going, but I do not agree with him. I know that his actions left a lasting impression on me, though, and made me realize that if I wanted to stay within the family, I would have to marry someone Jewish.

Julie and I started our trip the next day, with the blessing of my parents. We drove off toward our first stop, wherever that might be. We had everything we wanted in the car; a small bag of clothes, a cooler for snacks and drinks, some pot and even a little cocaine. (It was the 1980's, after all.) The coke was gone before we reached Mankato. I was kind of glad because the last thing I wanted to happen was to get pulled over and get busted for possession. Didn't worry about the pot, though. We had a great time on the trip. What I loved most about it was that there was no plotted course and we could go as we pleased. That was one of the greatest qualities I learned from Julie. Serendipity. We never had any reservations at any hotel and would either camp out or find a place to stay.

One night, we left Yellowstone National Park and were looking for a place. All the hotels were booked solid. I had stopped at a phone booth to make some calls to hotels (no cell phones in those days,) but there were no rooms to be found. We fought as I drove on this skinny, pitch-black road, in the middle of the Rockies. We could see nothing but the lights of my car lighting up the way, sometimes just dirt. For sure, we were lost in the middle of the night, in the middle of nowhere.

I said we should have planned better, but Julie was adamant about winging it. We pressed on and finally hit a city with a room. The last room available in someplace called Jackson Hole. Up in the attic, the door was made for a dwarf. Bending down, we walked into what looked like a large closet. We were just happy to be in a place with clean beds. We fell asleep right away.

The next morning, we woke up and looked out the window. There, right outside the hotel, were the Teton Mountains, majestic as anything I have ever seen. From the hotel, the mountains shot straight up, green with summer cover, flowers everywhere, one of the most beautiful sights I had ever encountered. Julie, I recall, said to me, "See, Lee, good things do happen to good people. You would have never booked a room with this kind of a view in this kind of a town." She was right.

We continued our journey through Tahoe and Reno and the sweetest little town called Carmel, before making our way down the incredible Coastal Highway 1 to Julie's sister in Los Angeles. She and her husband lived a very different lifestyle than I was used to, but I felt taken in very warmly. To me, what a life!

They lived in Beverly Hills, and had a wonderful home, two kids, and good friends. Everyone wanted to be with them. I thought *I could really see myself living this kind of life*. It looked so happy and fulfilling. They each had their separate lives, did what they each wanted. She would work out at home while he went to the newest and hottest workout centers. She had friends over for lunch and they'd go shopping. He'd meet friends or clients at a club for lunch. They'd meet at night and do their thing together, and then start the next day. Yep, what a marriage! I could do that. It looked like a good life.

We had a great time with them, but it was time to head off to Vegas. Last stop, and the best, because this was a classy city and you could get dressed up and go to nice dinners. We had been on the road for ten days already and we had been wearing the same clothes over and over again. It was going to be high-class fun now.

We pulled into the old MGM hotel. I told Julie to wait while I saw if they had a room. I went to the front desk and told the clerk that I had just gotten married and did not have a lot of money.

I asked if it were possible to get a nice room or suite so I could impress my wife. I guess I was lucky that we pulled into town on a Tuesday. He gave me the large honeymoon suite!

When Julie saw the room, she was very impressed and that was all that mattered to me. The room was huge, with an oversized bed and two vanities, two showers, two toilets and a large, sunken Jacuzzi tub surrounded by mirrors. This was going to be fun. *Ask me now if we had made love that moment or that night, I can't remember.* I hope we did, because it was one of the grandest suites we ever stayed in.

We got home a few days later. We had a great time. Sure, we had fights, but like I have always said, we had a lot more fun than not. It was a trip I never wanted to end. I had such a great time with Jules. We had talked non-stop the whole trip. We were rarely apart and I could not wait to wake up to see this beautiful person next to me each morning. I knew I wanted to be with her. She left an impression on me that no one had or has ever since.

A few days after we returned from our trip, I met her for dinner at the King's Inn. I could not stand being away from her. After the main course, I said, "Maybe we should get married." Julie looked at me and without hesitation said, "If you want to ask me to marry you, then you have to ask my mom." I said, "Alright, set it up." She did. I didn't ask her, or myself even, why she wanted me to ask her mom first. I thought that it was kind of strange considering their relationship. A few days later, I got off work, went home, showered really good, put on my black pants, off-white turtleneck shirt, sport coat over that and took off to change my life. Julie had said she could smell me coming around the corner since I put on almost a half a bottle of cologne.

I remember sitting at the kitchen table waiting for her mother to come in. She finally did. Oh my God! Here, this woman that I had always seen impeccably dressed and "done," even when gardening, walked into the kitchen in a robe with a blue mud face mask and hair in curlers under a plastic bag... This is the time I'm going to ask her permission to marry her youngest daughter?!

I said, "I'll get right to the point. I would like you to be my mother-in-law."

Oh my God! What did I just say?? Not exactly as I had been practicing, but I guess it's the way it came out, as the story goes. For the next two hours, Betty gave us every reason in the book why she did not want us to get married, but I don't recall any of them, because, frankly, I was not listening. When she finally exhausted herself, I got up and said, "Betty, I respect your wishes, but we are going to get married and as of this time, we are engaged."

There was something about Julie that made me feel different about a woman than I'd ever experienced before. But still, marriage was what was on my mind. I knew that's what I wanted and needed. Marriage was my goal. What I didn't know was what it takes to make a marriage work. I just knew that we belonged in each other's life somehow.

I was so glad when she finally agreed to marry me.

CHAPTER 1 DISCUSSION

Recognizing Our Own Blueprints

What makes us want to get married in the first place? To be loved and cared for? That's generally in there. To fit in, perhaps? To be part of a couple... We've all been the third wheel at some point, right? And, "young love" is so simple, sweet, and filled with fantasy. When it's blended with a true friendship, we may confuse true love with the ideology of creating a home and family with this wonderful person in whose presence, we seem to shine. Aristotle debated this and concluded that we have three most important relationships in life: our family, our friends, and our lovers. They should not be confused for the other. We should not expect any one person to fulfill all those roles and expect the relationship to last.

The American Dream is known the world over: marriage, children, pets, perfect jobs and home, vacations, education, meaningful volunteer work, retirement... We're trained to be part of the group, and live the myth of "Happily Ever After." Sometimes, even to be accepted within our own families, we find we must comply by these rules.

Yet, each of us has a uniqueness that, with self-esteem, shines. This shine may be too brilliant for the group, so we are told to dull it or be "outcast." Most of us, in our nubile stage of emotional development, attach to doing what we need to do to be accepted, thereby dulling our brilliance in favor of acceptance.

Pubescently, we might rebel, but often too long after our brilliance has been forgotten, and we flounder in our freedom. We find we must decide if we are going to take care of ourselves, or rely on and wait for others to help us. Usually, some "thing" happens to us that generates enough fear that we return, tail between legs, and succumb to do "what's right" in exchange for being part of the group. We decide to become worthy of the conditional love offered. We offer pieces of ourselves in exchange. To become "'worthy of love," we may begin to present ourselves in ways that are more acceptable. Men might take a date to a fancy dinner. Women might buy that push-up bra. Julie's mother always said, "A little powder, a little paint, makes a woman what she ain't." This in itself isn't bad; it's fun to be courting. Why do we feel the need to sell ourselves, hide our flaws and come off as the perfectly acceptable mate? We buy "acceptability" because it works for everyone else, right? Our self-deception begins and the seeds are planted. We are going to have the American Dream.

As our self-esteem wavers, our fear of more loss consumes us. We react to life, based on our fears controlling our mind. We make choices that are not in our "higher purpose's" best interests, and that leads to more loss of self-esteem from selling ourselves out. *For example: With a huge loss like the death of a parent, we lose our innocence, we learn that life is not forever. When our world is shaken, and our support system is weak, a loss of self-esteem easily follows. We react to life based on fears controlling our minds. It becomes a vicious circle... Or, is there a purpose to it all?*

<u>Evocations:</u>

1. What are my beliefs about marriage? Where did they come from?
2. What do I believe marriage will do for me? What will it not do?
3. What do I fear most about marriage? What do I look forward to?
4. What if my plans don't pan out? Would I still want to be mated with this soul?
5. What are you willing to sell of yourself in order to be loved or married? What do you expect of another to release of themselves in order for you to love or marry them?

* Interested in the origins of the words, husband or wife? (husbandry and waif)

CHAPTER TWO

Building the Vessel

Julie

The bets were on about how long our marriage would last *(or if we would even make it to the altar.)* That was enough to spur my rebelliousness. I would show everyone that I could be taken seriously, that I knew what I was doing and was going to put my all into it. Few thought I, a veritable sexpot, just on the brink of twenty years old, could, commit--or that Lee could keep me tamed and happy. How well others see us is interesting. How they present it is another issue. I've found over the years that when someone tells me I don't know what I'm doing or saying, it opens the floodgates of my stubborn, rebellious nature. C'est la vie, huh? Know thyself.

The week of the wedding was also the week of my 20th birthday. I had decided that if I were ever to have a daughter and she came to me at eighteen and said she was going to get married, I wanted to be able to tell her I had at least waited until I was twenty! (By five days, but who's counting?)

All the curses my mother threw at me, "Just you wait until you have a daughter of your own, you'll be sorry then!" *Uh, I don't think I'll put myself in that position, mommy dear. I'll lead my own life, and unlike you, I'll enjoy it. I won't blame my children for my misery or not doing what I wanted to do in life… I just wouldn't have any.*

Our wedding was right out of the movies, just as Lee's courting had been. He and his poor family had no idea what whirlwind of society agendas we'd be consumed with over the eleven months between our engagement and wedding. A couple weeks before the wedding (and months after the showers and bridal teas and other excuses for gala events with veiled hats and white gloves which replaced my fishnets and out-of-date-hippie clothing,) Lee and I had a serious talk where I told him I didn't think I could marry him in all honesty. Our sex life had not improved, but had actually become disenchanting.

I knew I loved him with all my heart, and wished it could work. I could see he would be such a good husband, and if I was really going to get married so young, he was the guy. But, it just wasn't clicking—the flame wasn't being fueled.

It was the first time of many that he chided me for putting sex so high on my list of priorities. He knew I realized that he would be a good husband, and I shouldn't worry about it. He said, "After the wedding, during our two-week honeymoon in Mexico, we'll put all our energies into it." Our honeymoon would be a perfect time to learn how to make love with one another, since we obviously hadn't figured it out during the first fourteen months of knowing each other intimately.

He was so persuasive. Did I really want to return all those gifts from all those parties in our honor? Did I really want to cancel all the upcoming events? How would we let everyone know in time?

Worst yet, did I really want to tell my family that they were right, that I had made a rash decision, and didn't know what I was doing? *WHAT WOULD EVERYONE SAY?* I might have acted like I didn't care, but it was bred into me.

Our wedding was right out of the movie, *"Goodbye Columbus."* We had 28 attendants for our black-tie event. It was the finest gala of my mother's career as 'Hostess-with-the-Mostest," so dubbed by a Minneapolis society writer on more than one occasion in her day.

After the signing of the Jewish marriage contract, our *Ketubah*, the Rabbi placed the veil over my head. I began to weep uncontrollably for a few moments, knowing that was 'it,' that I was already actually married. My mother told me that I could stop the ceremony there and then if I wasn't sure about it.

Looking back, I see she was giving me permission to back down from my stubborn, rebellious nature that screamed, *"I can do this. I'm a big girl!"* As scared as I was, I loved Lee and felt sure that we could make a good life together, side-by-side. I would have a family in him. At the time, however, I thought she was trying to prove, that by my crying, I had shown them all what a terrible mistake I was making. NO WAY! Not me! I was going to plunge in headfirst. Just watch us succeed!

The ceremony was achingly long, as we had to have two Cantors do their own version of the American Idol, proving each was a more proficient crooner than the other. One of our groomsmen passed out, having only ingested cocaine that day. Lee and I had promised each other we would be sober for the full day, until we got to the hotel and opened our champagne together. It didn't quite work out that way.

While everyone was ready to cut the cake and take pictures, Lee was nowhere to be found. Finally, he slinked into the room with a friend, wiping his nose and laughing cockily. I was fuming, but wasn't going to express it there in front of our entire reception. Better to wait until behind closed doors. It was 'the way' I learned to handle things. Why give gossipers fodder?

It was a very special day and night on so many levels. My family all got along so well, and for one magic day, they were all there for me, like it was supposed to be. I was finally in their group and accepted as an adult and peer and friend, it seemed. Although, one brother's toast was more of a roast on how he had caught me eating Lucky Charms and watching cartoons that very morning of my wedding.

"Is she really old enough to get married?" Oh, everyone loved that.

The crowd roared with laughter. It was the best production I had ever been in, although I still was horrified that my mother had gone ahead and hired a group to start "spontaneous Israeli dancing" in honor of my new Israeli in-laws, even though she had specifically promised me that it would not happen.

"I didn't think you'd notice, you'd be so busy having the best night of your life that I've paid for," was her response when I asked her why she lied to me. This was the kind of "truth" I was exposed to growing up. When I didn't let her off the hook with this one, she glared back at me, and called me an ungrateful, spoiled brat who didn't deserve such a wedding. I reminded her that this wedding was hers, not mine. I had nothing to do with any decision. She even placed all my friends at tables in another room after I had spent hours arranging them! We could have put a down payment on a huge house with what she spent just to ensure she would be invited to other's parties and events in return.

The only way out of that house was through marriage, unless I wanted to have her cut me entirely out of her life. It had already happened once. I knew her threats were real. I had lived outside her house when I returned from California. The school therapist suggested it would be better for us to make our daily efforts, and yet each have a place to go to when things got too rough. My mother wouldn't speak to me for months because I wasn't living at home. When I told her we were getting married, the only way she would participate was if I moved home for the year before our wedding. It was all power brokering... I'll support you if you do it my way, or I won't talk to you at all. *I am a glutton for punishment sometimes, I'll admit.*

All in all, Lee and I really did enjoy our wedding and had a wonderful time greeting all the tables, dancing cheek to cheek, getting roasted, and just enjoying our family and friends (and the extra 200 people there.) I did have to do some explaining to my friends about their having been seated in the other room. Even with that, my cheeks hurt from laughing and smiling so much all night long.

By the time the limo picked us up, we were exhausted. When we reached the hotel, we opened the bottle of Perrier-Jouet we received. Our aching feet, his throbbing head, and the sheer relief of it all being over were a few great excuses for each of us to not consummate the marriage that night. But I felt weird about it, like it was a bad omen.

The next morning, it was time to consummate. We'd ordered a sumptuous breakfast and had 45 minutes before it would show up. Perfect. Only, not. It was over way too soon, and when Lee walked away after having done "his part," I asked him where he was going. He said, "Well, I'm finished, but here, look, there's a mirror on the door, so keep going if you want... I'm going to shower. Have fun." And he promptly shut the door on me.

A silent scream was all I could respond—for the first 30 seconds.

Then I exploded, pounding on the bed, writhing in agony. "You LIAR! You tricked me! How could you make a promise to me that it would get better and yet this is the way you consummate our marriage? 'Here's a mirror?!' How dare you? There is NO WAY I am staying married to you. First, you go do cocaine when you said you wouldn't and I didn't say anything about it even, but this is NO WAY to start our marriage!"

He came out and sat down on the bed next to me. I could not allow him to comfort me from the wound he had just inflicted and the chain he had tricked me into wearing around my finger. He patted my back and asked me, "Are you really going to call it off, after everyone watched us make our vows yesterday and everything our parents have done for us? Over sex?"

He hit several nerves. Parents. My mother. How could I tell her I was so wrong, and she'd been so right? He watched the realization come over my eyes, then said, "Why don't we call them and thank them for everything they did for us. That would be the right thing to do. What are you going to do? Tell them you won't stay married to me because I didn't give you good enough sex on our first round of marriage?"

Which would be worse, confronting the conflict and dealing with the fallout, or simply sweeping it under the rug with all the other elephants? Lee was already picking up the phone and dialing while I lay there in a heap, trying to figure it out; unable to latch onto what was the right thing to do. We all make tough decisions each and every day. Whether we make a decision based on fear, or based on compassion, has much to do with the results affected by the decision.

He handed me the phone. It was his father. I'm supposed to call him Dad, now. I never called my own stepfather "Dad," the man who raised me to believe I was lovable those ten years, the man I never wanted to lie to for any reason. To Lee's Dad, I didn't exactly lie.

"What a perfect night, huh?" he said. I looked at the barely drunk champagne bottle, and answered him, "Best champagne I ever had." I wanted to run away.

My own deceptions had begun. I made my bed, and now I would have to lie in it, even if it would prove to be the loneliest bed I'd ever been in. Don't get me wrong. Lee and I were always such good friends that we were actually able to enjoy each other's company even though we'd have horrible disagreements. I thought that part was very healthy. We disagreed more than we agreed, I thought. Lee disagreed.

One issue for us was money. I really had no problem splurging when there was extra money around, but Lee had no future thought about money, credit, or a retirement plan. I knew we were young, but if we wanted to live the lifestyle he was into, then we needed to do some financial planning. He would just go buy something and put it on credit, saying we'll get a bonus in a few months and that'll pay for it. Except, there would be one bonus for every few times he would say that, so he didn't understand about budgeting. After having my credit card taken from me one day, I resolved no one would ever put me in that position again. I would be in charge of my own finances. Once I took over the bills, I finally reduced our debt to zero and started a savings plan. I was in Real Estate and knew what a person's credit report meant.

Despite our differences, I loved being with him, most of the time. He could make me laugh when I really didn't want to. He could also make me cry. What did I know of relationships? My mother always complained to me about my stepfather, whom I idolized. She told me that she only married him so I could have a father. How mèan! Did she tell him the same thing? I shudder to think it. But I also know it was so she had someone to go with to her events and parties...*They always fought about it, because he really didn't want to go to the theater or symphony. He would rather play cards with his buddies. Eventually, their love grew into something real.*

People I worked and played with for years would joke about my 'invisible husband' and how they didn't really believe I was married. I learned that if I wanted to go to a party, I needed to go alone. It didn't matter that I tried to be involved in his life, and all his family weekends at the cabin, or business parties. He was happy to have me next to him at all times when we were in a crowd. "Don't leave me alone" was his motto.

What about all the times I went alone with no one at my side?

Well, I couldn't wait around for him to change. I went and enjoyed myself whenever I could, as long as it never conflicted with one of his family gatherings. For the first ten years of our marriage, that is.

Ultimately, I let him go to things alone. I even stopped going down to Florida to see his parents after a hurtful conversation that mentioned my stepfather in an unkind way. I wasn't producing grandchildren or living the way a good wife should either, and they were not pleased with me anymore. It was no longer acceptable for me to break the rules. I should be in the kitchen, and with children.

Lee wanted to make me happy. Or so he kept telling me. His words did not match his actions, once again. I didn't want jewelry, an expensive bike or car, or even a bigger house or more clothes; I just wanted him to *want to* share the world with me—and not just the world his parents expected him to live in. And I wanted him to make love to me and with me, as an expression and exploration of our love.

The way I saw it, there were three options. Either there was something wrong with him physically, or I just didn't turn him on, or he was gay. None of those felt good to me. None gave me any control over my life if I stayed married to him. When I asked him about it, he told me, "This is all in your head. There's nothing wrong with our life. You're just looking for something to say is wrong, so it's about sex again. You need to learn how to be satisfied with life. You're always looking at what's wrong, and never at what's right!"

Was it really all in my head? Just what were my priorities, anyways? And were they mine, or some imposed socio-Judeo values? I found out that the only way an orthodox Jewish woman could ask for a divorce was to prove that her husband could not satisfy her at least twice a month. Twice a month? Who gets that?!? We would go months without anything but wrestling to get rid of my sexual energies. I was very good at wrestling, and I was known to be able to put almost any man on his back or knock them off their feet.

Lee didn't get the pent-up sexual energy I had, and I'm sure my beating him at wrestling was somewhat of an emasculation. I would have easily succumbed if I could release my energies normally. But he made me feel that I was the one that was abnormal. And my drive was becoming abnormal, as it was starved, and it bloated outward like a famished child's stomach.

It made me feel like I was crazy and downright mean. I couldn't believe some of the things that were coming out of my mouth, just to try to knock some sense into him and give this marriage a fair shot.

At one point, on a cruise, I started to arrange our cabin by putting the two tiny little beds together. He freaked that I was changing the look of the room or something to that effect. I looked at him and said, "Lee, honey, this is not a marriage. We are like brother and sister, not husband and wife or even close to lovers."

He was horribly hurt that I would say something so mean. It was absolutely a much better relationship than a brother/sister thing, he said. I had to agree. Though we had different interests, friends, goals and drives, we loved each other deeply. I loved being with him on so many levels. Dancing with him was so much fun, once he had a couple drinks to loosen up. It helped when others were on the dance floor, too. Even though we thought so differently, I loved talking with him.

One woman in our society, whenever she would see us anywhere, would come up to us while we'd be talking amongst ourselves. She would always say, "You two are always so engaged in whispering to each other! What can you possibly have to converse about all the time? Do you ever run out of things to say?" *She still says it to this day!*

We felt bad for her that she didn't have that relationship in her life, someone she never ran out of things to say to or engage with one another. We had witnessed older couples who sat in restaurants, never saying a word to one another. It didn't appear to be a Zen practice of silence, or meditating on the food. It was more of an "I'm sick and tired of having meals with this person with whom I have absolutely nothing mutually interesting or stimulating to discuss." We realized how fortunate we were to have the relationship we had. We joked that we had 90% of what it takes to have a perfect marriage. I thought I could handle his lack of presence in my life, but my resentments and temper gradually seeded deeper and stronger. Why wouldn't he travel with me, or try new restaurants? Why wouldn't he socialize with me? Why wouldn't he go see a doctor?

I asked Lee to see a doctor, to just get a simple blood test to see if there was something physically wrong with him. Instead, he'd change for a while; make an effort to go out to a new restaurant or to a party or have sex, maybe three efforts one week and then nothing for three months, and so it went. He'd also go through periods of trying to be involved in my interests and activities, just to let that drop as well. Various efforts over the years had various lengths of duration. I felt trapped in a practically sexless marriage. I had to rein in my own sexuality. But more and more, I was attracted to other men, men whose pheromones literally sucked my own from out of the depths. A few times, I couldn't control the flood of desire that drove me to do things I didn't want to think of myself as capable of doing. I didn't get married to become an adulteress.

But, it wasn't only the sex. We had major differences in what we wanted out of life—I wanted to see the world and learn all that it had to offer. Going to Las Vegas again for the umpteenth time, to the same restaurants, and the same shows made him happy and comfortable. For me, it became so redundant and predictable. Don't get me wrong, I'm not above gambling or having favorite destinations. It was just that, over the eight years, the lack of partnership had become exacerbated by the lack of the sexual glue that helps keep so many marriages intact. Starving for both levels of intimacy left me wandering on my own in a landscape that no longer fit the 'happily ever after' picture I had painted us to live in. I knew life would have its challenges, but being married was supposed to give you support through those hard times, wasn't it?

All of the sudden, he wanted children. For some reason, I agreed to try to get pregnant. We'd been married almost eight years and not having a child made me very abnormal to his family. Our sister-in-law already had three children, looked perfect all the time, and had a perfect home, even at 7:30 in the morning. His parents were no longer enamored with me--I was none of these things. I was not the perfect daughter-in-law because I had not produced children and had no plans of doing so. Every mother's day, I would get a negligee from his mother, in hopes that it would add the spice for me to entice him to get me pregnant. She didn't realize that he preferred long flannels, with pants and a bathrobe. Less intimidating.

Once I agreed to try to get pregnant, Lee became very interested in sex. We spent the summer trying and not succeeding, but at least I didn't have to argue with him to get any. "Honey, my temperature is just right...." was all I had to say.

But something still felt weird about it all. At first, there was the glow of newfound sexuality that had risen once again. But, eventually, it became the duty.

Finally, I lost it. I told him, "The greatest insult to me yet in our sex life, is that you are now making love to me to satisfy your parents. I'm not going to continue this. If you need children, you'll need to find another wife. I'm not going to lock myself into a marriage with a man who doesn't desire me--other than to please his parents."

That week of our eighth anniversary, we almost split up.

When he returned home from a business trip with his parents later that week, he told me I was right about everything. He was trying to please his parents and they didn't care about me as myself but as a baby producer not doing her job. He told me I'd given him the best eight years of his life and that he remembered we agreed to not having children when we got married. He realized he wanted to spend our lives together, traveling and learning, and experiencing new things.

He was going to get a vasectomy, next week.

That night we made love passionately. It was as though our entire life was ahead of us and we were back to that place of being life partners, there for one another, through thick and thin, creating our own version of 'happily ever after.'

Right in the midst of our lovemaking, the condom shredded into a thousand pieces. I'd never seen anything like it before in my life. I was horrified and ran into the bathroom. I jumped in the tub and turned on the spray, trying to clean myself out before any sperm got inside. I suddenly threw the sprayer down, realizing I had just thrust those sperm in even deeper. Something had happened. I felt the connection. I was paralyzed and started crying, hyperventilating. All I could say was, "Oh, my God! Oh, my God!"

Lee laughed it off as nothing. I was crazy, he said.

I'd never gotten pregnant in all the times we tried, so why would I worry about it this time? But I had a sinking feeling that what I knew was correct. When I confessed my fears to Lee, he laughed it off nonchalantly and said, "Well, we just decided we weren't going to have children, so we just won't have it. Relax."

RELAX?! I wasn't some unwed teenage girl. I had a fairly good marriage to a good man, a wonderful home and dog and lifestyle. I loved what my life had promised to be with my husband's new vows to me. We were going to see the world together. But how could I turn away a soul that chose us, against the odds, to come to us at the last possible moment?

A month went by.

I knew I was most definitely pregnant.

Lee - 2

I do remember telling Julie I wasn't going to get drunk or anything at our wedding. Of course, I didn't drink. But, yeah, I did do some drugs in the bathroom during the reception. It was the 80's, it was a different time. How old was I? Twenty-three years old? I mean it was dumb, it was stupid, selfish, and it was without thought. Yeah, I have a lot of regret for that night, for that evening—even though it was a beautiful, beautiful ceremony and reception party.

When we got married, we were young and in love. Julie and I were soul mates; destined to spend the rest of our lives together. I had no idea the amount of work and energy it would take to make a marriage work, mentally, emotionally, sexually, just how encompassing it is. Julie was very intimidating sexually; an aggressive girl, definitely different from anyone else I'd ever dated, or had a sexual experience with.

I did not know what sex was supposed to be like. The only thing I knew about how sex was supposed to be was from the kind of sex I'd been having. Like every boy in America, I learned everything from the book, *"Joy of Sex."* It didn't really explain about intimacy, you know; it just showed a lot of different positions. It didn't explain about what the woman was supposed to have, what the man was supposed to have. It didn't tell you of prolonging and multitudes of the female orgasm (*at least not underneath the pictures.*)

During the seventeen years we were together, our marriage seemed fine to me. I was very happy. I enjoyed being married to Jules, and in my eyes, we lived almost the perfect life. She is a beautiful person, full of passion for life, seeking to learn as much about it as there is to learn. God, I could kick myself in the ass for not doing more things that she wanted to do. It was a stage; it was a personality trait of mine that no matter what she wanted to do, I would say, "No."

There were sometimes where I would go out and party with her, and we would have a ball, a gas, the absolute best time, but it would still not sink into my head. The next time around I would say, "No, I'm going to stay home and watch basketball,"...baseball, football... whatever excuse I could come up with not to go with her for some odd reason, it didn't matter what it was. I don't have an explanation, even to this day. It's just a very strange thing.

I know I was a very closed person. I always needed to be pushed to get out and experience life. Julie loved meeting people; I hated having people over. I was involved with the family business, and I worked a lot.

My father came from a very strict background. He is a dominating person and instilled in me a very strong work ethic. "Business first, family second." From what I could see, this was how you lived your life. I would have loved to travel with Julie, but I was scared of what my father would think.

No way would I admit this to Julie. So many times, my father would say, "In business and in life, you do not share everything with your wife." Of course, I told her things and before family gatherings, I would brief her about what my father and brother thought she didn't know.

I hated it, but it was the way I was.

Balancing the kind of open and honest relationship Julie wanted with keeping loyal to my father's beliefs put a strain not only on our marriage, but also on my life and the way I acted. Julie began having friends over only when I was at work or out of town just because I was so uncomfortable with it. She would tell them I was due home around 5:00, at which time they would scatter away. Julie walked on eggshells, hoping they would be gone before I arrived home. Then she would have to scramble to make everything spotless again. My house was my castle.

This was another thing I learned from my father. I wanted to come home from work, hang with Julie, turn on the TV and veg until it was time for bed.

Time for bed... How many times did I do whatever I could to make sure we didn't go to bed together? Sex was our biggest issue.

Coming from a home where nobody ever talked about sex or made it seem a part of marriage, I thought it was something for the man rather than the woman. Then I married a woman who was very sexual. She knew that sex was not a duty to fulfill, but an emotional experience where two become one.

Julie would literally throw herself at me. I was stumped. How could I not want her? How could I lie in bed next to this voluptuous woman who wanted me and not take what was offered?

There was just no way, with the kind of mentality that I had, to discuss any of this with my friends. I wasn't open. I wasn't forthright with information about myself, so there was no way in the world that I was going to discuss this.

I didn't have a strong sex drive; Julie did. I wanted to make her happy, but I couldn't. It wasn't that I didn't love her. I loved her deeply. Our strong bond was probably what kept us together for so long. She kept asking me to see a doctor. To this day, I don't know why I didn't. I knew there was something wrong. We might have been able to overcome our differences.

We were so different from other couples on so many levels. The bills were yet another role reversal for us. The first couple of years, I naturally did the bills because that is what a man does. But, if I didn't feel like doing them, I didn't. That was my prerogative. It took one time of Julie having her credit card taken away from her at Dayton's (Okay, it was in front of our sister-in-law and nephew,) before she stormed in and took all monies into her own hands. I would give her my check and I'd get a stipend – $190! She'd get ALL the rest! I don't know what she did with it all... I do know that I couldn't do much with that for two weeks! I couldn't even buy a shirt, one of the things I LOVED to buy. I brought the money home... it didn't seem very fair. I guess we did have pretty good credit and savings by the time we split up, but still...

After our divorce, well, what was left over from my check, and it was A LOT, I went out and bought shirts, because I could. Ties, pants, shoes, and cufflinks, too. If I liked it, I bought it. It was fun and exciting to make all these decisions and purchases without having someone look over my shoulder.

Another difference in our marriage compared to those I witnessed and used as a frame of reference, was the issue of children. Julie and I did discuss having kids before we got married, and we definitely made a decision that we were not having children. I was all right with it. There was always the thought that maybe one day she would change her mind—and I would be okay with that too. Then the pressures from my parents wanting more grandchildren started to weigh in. There were definitely pressures, and not just from them.

Maybe the period where we actually did try to have a baby was just Julie trying to make me happier. We did have some incredible sex. Maybe subconsciously it was her way of, you know, to get me to want to have sex with her. It was one of those scenarios where you decide you don't want to have kids. Then you change your mind and try to have kids, but you can't. Then you decide again that you won't have them. And then, BOOM!

CHAPTER 2 DISCUSSION
Recognizing the Building Materials

Often, people find a spouse that emulates their opposite gender parent and subconsciously expect that spouse to carry out that parent's role in their life. To find their perfect "Prince/ss Charming," some prefer bars or special interests to internet match services or being fixed up. Whichever way we go out and 'sell ourselves' on the 'market' is also how we do our own shopping. We shop for the one who could make our dreams come true, and sell ourselves as the one to make theirs come true. I don't mean this toward any one or group; this is what we are bombarded with constantly in today's media-filled society. Everywhere you look, there is advertising, and for the last 100 years, it has sold 'normalcy.' But, most of us are unique, even though we are made of the same elements.

We each choose paths on which to learn our life's lessons. The Humanistic Psychologist Abraham Maslow defined a famous "Hierarchy of Needs:"

Self-Actualization (enlightenment)
Esteem Needs (worthiness)
Belonging Needs (companionship)
Safety Needs (shelter and protection)
Physiological Needs (food, water, air)

We cannot move higher on the ladder until we have fulfilled the needs on the lower rungs. Without recognizing our current level of need, we search for the level we may have missed growing up; which could include someone to pay the bills or that has ambition or has a desire to release negative emotions. Add that to the opposition of finding someone who emulates our opposite gender parent, and BANG! We're 'in love.'

Others might wallow in how they lost the "one and only'" and will never find their "true love" again, or maybe some wonder why their soul mate hasn't shown up, but perhaps will settle for the next best person that comes along.

Harsh?

Perhaps, but how many of you reading this don't know anyone whose marriage was based on, "Well, my time is running out and there's no one better" or "They are exactly what I always knew I would marry... " or for whatever reason somehow did not see the red flags that they were setting themselves up for their own self-designed prison. And, how many of those folks blame their spouse for being who they are, versus who we wanted them to be? *If it wasn't for… then I'd be happy.*

If we have taken Psych 101, or any type of therapy, we know we can't expect others to change, any more than we want them to expect us to change. But, we do sacrifice pieces of ourselves to maintain harmony. Which parts do we pick to release? To be in a relationship, compromises are a necessity and must be maintained on various levels to create enjoyment of the world together.

Perhaps, we begin to realize what beliefs we have that may be different than our parents' or the social context in which we grew up. So, how do our own beliefs and values fit into this pre-designed life? We've been, figuratively, and sometimes literally, asked to "sell out" on our ideals, but we want to, against the odds, triumph in our idealism of what we've come to believe is important in this new day and age. We will make this marriage work on better terms than what we learned!

Evocations:

1. What did I get from my opposite gender parent, and what did I not get?
2. Upon what did I really base my decision in choosing my spouse?
3. What deceptions of myself did I allow, and why?
4. What red flags did I choose to ignore, in order to persist with my plan?

CHAPTER THREE

Surviving the Doldrums, Riding the Trade Winds

Julie

I was terrified of being a mother and perpetuating the mother-daughter patterns I knew. I wanted to be as good a mother as I could, without losing myself, or my own identity. Tasha was amazing. God knew I needed an easy baby and Tasha was more than that. She was a delight. She didn't cry for the first four months of her life, barely. She *cooed* and *ooo'd* watching everything that she could focus on for such long periods of time. She was an old soul that honored us with her presence. I believe she also came to teach me much about love, life, and myself. I needed to examine who I really wanted to be, and who I really wanted to teach her to be… I had to look myself in the mirror and admit some of her naughty habits were mine.

At around two-and-a-half years old, Tasha was pulling that typical bedtime rig amoral, "Another glass of water… another story… another song… another hug and kiss"… I finally said, "No more, my girl. Mommy still has work to finish and it is late." I got up to leave, but she wanted to tell me one more thing. I said, "No more."

She said, "I want to tell you how I got in your tummy."

I sank down on the edge of her bed, "I'm listening…"

She proceeded to tell me she had a very hard time getting in, and that she had to "Say a special magic prayer" which put a key in her hand. She was told that once she got in, she had to lock the door behind her and throw the key away so she wouldn't fall out…"

I trembled, dumbfounded. "Who told you to lock the door, Sweetpea?"

She mumbled something. She was finally asleep. Me? I was whacked out for the next few hours! I knew she had come to us at what seemed like the last possible moment, even though Lee never got a vasectomy until a few years after she was born. This confirmed for me that she was such a blessing in our lives. Still, the lessons I had to learn through my girl being in my life were rigorous, to say the least. I had much un-learning to do. I took that story as one of cosmic significance.

I knew she had powers of memory or insight that always surprised me.

Our daughter became the love of Lee's life, and I was often on the sidelines of this incredible relationship that I supported for them. I ached for attention from each of them, getting only morsels when being traded for some kind of exchange. Tasha would be able to show affection to Lee, but she had a very tough time showing it to me. She would actually catch herself if she was being cuddly, kissy or touchy with me, and then she would stop herself. I felt like it was learned behavior from her dad. Not all the time, but definitely when Lee was around. When he'd be gone for a couple weeks, she and I would have more affectionate times. We had tickle time every night when he was gone. Neither of them could give me too much, though. I definitely had jealous feelings.

We led what seemed a perfect life but still had problems. I began to feel that my life was only about giving myself to them and their every need, but that they felt no need to replenish me. I needed to figure out how to do that on my own.

In my opinion, sexuality is about more than an orgasmic release, although I think that released combustion is one of the 're-boot' buttons our body has. Like a great laugh or cry, or spectacular nap leaves one entirely drained of built-up or pent-up, chaotic energy, which is replaced with a freshly charged battery. Afterwards, we are calmer, clearer and have a certain glow about us. Sexuality is about connection with another, rejuvenation, revitalization, and pleasurable loving. I had a couple affairs over the years, one that made me think I was ready to leave Lee. Eventually, it made me realize that no one would love me the way he did, nor allow me to do whatever I wanted, even if that meant doing what I wanted to do alone.

Consequently, I immersed myself in anything that interested me. My Real Estate career had never really satisfied me, but I got so much flack about being such a gypsy, that I eventually stuck with it for over 19 years. On the other hand, my gypsy nature kept me interested in many areas outside of my work.

I finally applied for massage school. There, I connected with my own psychic abilities of laying my hands on people. It wasn't sexual at all, it was simply connecting with another body and allowing my senses to know what was needed to help them. Helping people inspired me to continue my studies. I knew I was going to have another number of careers that would deal with healing.

My Real Estate income allowed me to study Chinese Medicine, Homeopathy, Shamanism, Yoga and several other modalities of healing over the years. Lee would always roll his eyes at my latest, greatest discovery of truths I was bringing into our home. I would slip in some of the nutritional supplements or homeopathic remedies, which he couldn't deny worked. In fact, if he or some of my friends would be feeling ill or under the weather, they would jokingly say, call 'dr. Jules.' Lee and I did put to practice many of those philosophical theories into our communications, *when he was in the mood.*

We were attempting to incorporate and apply some of the thought processes I had been studying through Taoism, Buddhism and linking those to Judaism. The very nature of nature is that all things will change; that anything that begins a life, lives its duration and then dies or returns to dust; that clinging to that which must change causes suffering; and hugely, *that what we plant, we shall reap... that one crosses all divinities.*

Years went by. We actually saw a few therapists, counselors, and I even got him to see a psychic. The trained therapists and counselors that we chose weren't able to quite put their hands around our issues. We were an enigma. The MMPI personality tests we took explained many things in our relationship, but weren't able to quite get to the core of our problems. They were validating in particular areas but weren't really illuminating any epiphanies for us.

The psychic told us the visions she saw when thinking of us was that of *"two pilings driven so deeply into the earth that it would take a natural disaster like a hurricane to tear down the structures"* built upon those pilings, our foundation. This triggered both of us to remember the significance of our cosmic relationship. We had always wanted to believe that our love would conquer all our problems, first and foremost.

I joined him on a business trip over Valentine's Day, our half-year anniversary of our 14th or 15th year of marriage. We had a beautiful night in Las Vegas. He had naturally won at the high stakes and he bought me new, expensive clothes. We bought new wedding bands, champagne, caviar and candles. We had cosmic, body-melting/merging, mind-blowing sex! When we *did connect*, it was great.

We renewed our vows that lovely evening.

It was a dream come true, until I blew it. I asked Lee to make one last vow—that he would be willing to work on our sex life so we could share this more often. I couldn't just let it be what it was for the moment, but the moment was monumental—we were renewing our vows. He said he was too tired to make one more vow.

Not even just a few words?...

No, he was going to go to sleep now.

I couldn't get in bed with him. My fury was rising. I lit a cigarette in the dark.

He said, "Oh, I'll have one, too."

He was awake enough to smoke, but not to make a one-sentence vow to me???!!! I threw the pack of cigarettes at him. I was seething with hurt and anger.

I told him he was driving me away and that if I found a man that loved me the way he did AND wanted to *make* love to me, I was going to grab it. I had hoped this would knock some sense into Lee… since he knew that I had already been unfaithful.

Instead, he told me he would *understand when that happened!* Case closed.

Due to our obvious, re-occuring problems, Lee and I spoke many times over the years about if we ever divorced, how we would want to handle it.

One thing we recognized in our dance of anger, blame, and shame interspersed with fun, love and comfort, was our pattern of 'energy play.' Through massage school, I found I was very much susceptible to the energy people put out. Lee would come home after an extremely difficult day and pick a fight with me until I would burst into battle feeling backed into a wall so hard that I would have to become offensive to get off the defensive. As soon as I took on his negative energy, it was as if I was a conduit for him and he would release it and feel much better, immediately! It took us years to figure that one out, but it still comes into play, *even as we write this book*.

The summer before Lee and I finally did divorce was a very difficult one. Lee was extremely irritable and demanding, sometimes downright mean…*once in a while, actually verbally abusive.* I didn't know what was going on with him, and every time I would bring up the subject, I would get my head bitten off. He would tell me that it was all in my head, talking to me with disdain painted all over his face. I asked if it was about the affairs he had found out about. He wouldn't discuss it.

One day, after weeks of these tirades, he was so out of line and hurtful that even he couldn't help but recognize how cruel he had just been. I was crushed, but hopeful when he admitted he could no longer deny his outbursts. He was willing to talk, to communicate right now. This was big. The door finally opened and I asked him again what was eating at him to make him spew his venom so strongly at me.

He confessed to me that he felt it was in my best interest to finally leave him, to get off the fence of wondering if we could ever have a real marriage bed, or for him to share my life as well. He felt there was no way I would ever be satisfied, but he knew I would never leave him unless I hated him.

So, for my best interest, he was trying his best to actually make me hate him.

My love for Lee, during all of our life together, was real. *It still is.*

There were times when I wanted or needed to hate him. However, I learned that this hate actually stemmed from fear that I was not truly loved or lovable, as I was. If I was, then *why did my family issues continuously deal with abandonment?* My husband was there for me to a certain degree--if I supported his life and his happiness.

My response to learning his thoughts about me needing to hate him was that I loved him through all the thick and thin we had been through, and that if we ever did separate, I hoped we could do so lovingly, compassionately and ethically. I said, "Why would we ever want to hate each other? The one we thought would make our life perfect? So, we're not perfect. I still love you, perfect or not. That doesn't mean I can be married to you, though, if you aren't willing to work on our marriage fully."

We set a six-month timeframe within which we would give our marriage "it all." We finally saw a sex therapist, at the Department of Human Sexuality. Our experienced sex therapist seemed, to me, to have never even had sex. This therapist happened to resemble Pat from Saturday Night Live (the androgynous character who no one can tell if he's a she, or she's a he.) S/he tells us it is natural to have different drives. I think this person has never had a drive and had no clue what I was talking about, especially since both their eyes obviously glazed over when I described my thoughts on sexuality.

Eventually, the last straw hits, when one night Lee tells me, "Take it or leave it. I'm done working on it." With that, I got a pillow and slept on the couch again while he went to our bed. I never let myself be naked in front of him again. He never once commented on it; *he was relieved.*

The six-month deadline was missed as I continued to prepare to move by getting finances and household things into place. Lee acted as if nothing was going on except for a little joke here and there, "Oh, I guess if you ever move out you could take this, and I'll get a new one."

He would always tell me, "I say what I mean." As a result, that's precisely what I did. I packed up dishes and towels, and went out and bought new ones for him. Every movement towards moving out, I questioned why I would leave a perfect life over sex. *Except, it wasn't just sex.* The lack of intimacy spread, it seeped into all these other areas and there was no relief of the tension that would build up between us.

He had said several times, "You're going to leave me one day anyway, so why bother?" I never could reconcile 'why bother?' Wasn't I worth it? Wasn't our marriage worth bothering for? I was still waiting for Lee to realize that I was serious and say, "Stop sweetie, let's work this out." It never happened.

Instead, right in the midst of one of my rituals, *as I was sitting on an animal skin rug in lotus position, surrounded by drums, rattles, wands, dream catchers, and crystals, lighting another candle, throwing tobacco in the air and rubbing dark stones over my chakras in a counter-clockwise motion asking all the totems and spirits of my ancestors and the land to come forth, while questioning my tarot cards on what to do,* my phone rang with a call from the universe. My friend had won a contest at work, and the prize? Two free tickets to the Cayman Islands for the following week. We both wanted to know, *could I go?!!*

A few weeks earlier during a similar ritual, I forgot the word healthy when I asked God to send a man to love me. Love and passion showed up… before I had actually moved out.

Through serendipitous events, I met Oscar, a treasure-hunting sea captain in the Caribbean. The first night Oscar and I hung out together, we danced as if we were professionals: anticipating the other's moves and finishing with a flourishing dip to the crowd's cheers. We walked down to the beach and sat in the sand as he taught me about the constellations in the sky. We laughed and discussed philosophy for hours. He teased that I was somehow making him break all the rules, the first one being no married tourists except on their last night-*I had four more nights.* He said that it was "the passion for life" in my eyes that made him break the rule. He dropped my friend and I at our hotel, I kissed him on the cheek and thanked him for the best evening I had in such a long time.

He was impressed that I left it at that. So was I.

He more than insisted on taking on any and all tour guide responsibilities from that point forward. The next day he drove my friend and me to Rum Point Beach on the other side of the island. I took the place in with total awe triggering all my senses; it was delicious, right out of a movie set. The painted sky, the white sand beach, the water so blue and clear you could see the bottom sand rippling hundreds of feet from shore. It was the most serene and beautiful place I'd ever seen, *in a touristy way.*

We rented jet skis. I'd always been very afraid of them but at this point in my life, I was challenging myself not to be afraid of things, to live my life fully and not be afraid of death. I had to face my fears in the wide-open ocean. I'm not a thrill seeker, but once on that Jet Ski, I became fearless. I rode it as if I was a bucking bronco or a racecar driver. To have this unbridled power, it was thrilling, exhilarating, and scary. I finally understood why people like rollercoaster rides.

Later, I was lying on a hammock, swinging in the breeze under palm trees and parrots, watching the iguanas. I was feeling a bit delirious, probably from alcohol poisoning; we'd been drinking so much. Also, we were falling deliriously in love, yet, I was detached from the outcome. I knew this was all a fantasy, and that I had a reality coming up that wouldn't be so... enlivening.

I was going to enjoy what life I could while I was here.

Oscar walked up with cocktails for each of us and we laid head to toe facing one another. The breeze tickled over our flesh. I believed that I had found paradise. Truths and life's heartaches were exposed with every sip of punch. Oscar and I talked for hours. He spoke of what he thought about his life and what he still wanted to do, in his dreams. He spoke about his son that he had left in Venezuela, and how all he wanted in the world was to be with him. *He had all the excuses that we all make up for ourselves—about why we can't do something that we say we want to.* There was something so wretched in that, and I felt his pain. He told me things he'd never told anyone before. He didn't know why he was opening up so honestly with me, but he said he was inspired by me.

I convinced Oscar he should reunite with his son, because the pain he experienced from his own childhood abandonment was being repeated. His mother left him alone with his younger sister and brother when he was four years old. It was five days before a neighbor found them and called his father! The rest of his life was spent going from his grandparents to his father's new wife's to military school.

Oscar had married his wife at the height of his career, but when the coup he was in to overthrow the Venezuelan government failed, he was jailed as a traitor. After the second coup was victorious, he was released from prison, and his military post. His family life fell apart in that wake. He left, having all his things thrown out. He was offered a job as a mercenary. Thankfully, someone else offered him a job hunting treasure, and captaining boats in between those jobs. Subsequently, here he was, running boats in the Caribbean. Not bad, and better than a mercenary!

In witnessing his pain, I realized that I could not just leave my family entirely for the damage it would produce. I must find a way to preserve our family without being married to Lee.

Oscar, with a well-hidden mental illness, saw me as his last chance for a fulfilling life.

My flight home was in the morning. On our last night, as I lay wrapped in Oscar's arms, tears filled my eyes. "What is it?" he asked with deep concern. I looked into his bluest of blue eyes and explained, "I have loved Lee for so long and have tried so hard to make it work between us, but he doesn't believe that this is possible."

Confused, Oscar said, "So you cry because you wish I were him?" I explained, "No Oscar, I am mourning the loss of the dream that I could ever have this with him."

After a few satiating days of intimacy and heart wrenching talks, I realized what was missing in my marriage was real. Oscar had reignited in me pieces that had been so doused I didn't even know they were still there. He found all these treasures inside of me, which had been tucked so far away, hidden underneath the folds of my fears and "what-if's."

Whether or not I would ever see Oscar again, I resolved to never be an adulterer again. I knew I was going home to end my marriage.

Lee and I had not touched or kissed one another in four months other than a peck on the cheek: a good-bye, have-a-good-day, love-you kind of kiss. We hadn't kissed like lovers or husband and wife since Thanksgiving. It was now March.

I came home probably still smelling of Oscar. *Rude...*

Lee and I tagged off. We had one night together before he left for a week on a business trip. We had sex and it was so lackluster, it was so dutiful, so "let's get it over with." I cried and cried, and he didn't even notice. I didn't say anything because it was the biggest trip of the year for their sales team.

I wasn't about to take the whole company down with one of the lead men having just found out his wife was leaving him that day. Even so, I was never surer about it—I could never spend another night in bed with this man, my husband, *or anyone* that I didn't feel wanted to be there next to *me*, vs. just a body. I could never do it to myself again. *Never is a long time, isn't it?*

Asking Lee for a divorce came after many years of trying hard to make our marriage work. Honestly, there were plenty of reasons we stayed married for so long. We did have a beautiful life on many levels. We were family and loved one another in that way. We kept gradually working on the particular problems of the season. Eventually some got better. However, some got worse.

During the first seven to ten years, one of my biggest fears was that everyone who came to my wedding had been right to tell me I shouldn't get married so young. The next years of my marriage, the fear was that if I left Lee, I would be giving up the best thing in my life--my family. Additionally, I worried what would happen to Lee and Tasha if I left him… I knew he was still vulnerable to falling into a darkness that would pervade not only his, but Tasha's life, as well. For many years, I worried he would be buried alive by it.

Still, in all my lunatic studies, he did pick up on learning to catch himself more quickly during those moments of panic or rage. Although he had stood up to my mother when he wanted to marry me, I had yet to see him ever stand up to his father. Lee was still very controlled by him, even at 40 years old. I now knew he would be able to stand on his own legs with his family, at this point. *He did have a little pendulum swing to go through first, though.*

Lee left town on his business trip, and I had a whole week to re-connect with Tasha, as well as figure out how, when and just what I was going to say to him, and, not to mention, *catch up on all my work.*

During that week, Oscar wrote to me. I remember that every cell in my body was thrilled to hear from him, that he had made the effort to tell me he loved me more each day. He told me that he had vacation time coming up and wanted to come see me. My mouth droped, and I told him it was a very different world in Minneapolis than it is in the Cayman Islands. I tried to explain that I had a whole life going on up here as a mother, as a woman who was about to get a divorce, as a businesswoman in the busiest time of the year. Not to mention, a Jewish woman who was about to have a Passover Seder for her immediate family--thirty people. It was not a good time.

But for him *to come up in the winter*, oh, but he loved the snow. He had only seen it once. He so wanted to be here. He'd help me cook for the Seder! He waxed and waned so beautifully. His words took me in, mingling with the endorphins and that high of being in love.

Oh God! I still needed to talk to Lee. I needed to move out of my house. I needed to do all sorts of things, but I was missing and needing Oscar and somehow or another I found it in myself to say, "Okay, come."

By the end of the conversation, I was just as involved in the scheme as he was. I was ready for a change in my life because I felt so dead. It was going to be a scandal, but I thought I was prepared for it.

Lee returned from his business trip on such a high. I knew I was going to be taking him down, bad. I also knew it had to be done. I spent the entire day trying to write a letter to him over and over. How was I to tell him that I loved him but couldn't be married to him? I knew that this had to be done in the calmest of manners and in the gentlest, most loving way.

When I first handed Lee the letter, he pushed it away. I watched him as he read it; the shock, dismay, then anger that registered in him. Lee glared at me, and then, when the ramifications of his words and actions were squarely in front of him, then he started bargaining. He said, "No, no, no, let's try a separation."

We had made a decision seven months earlier that we weren't going to separate. We hadn't seen any separations that cured anything, whether people got back together or not. He had always bargained but the problem in my eyes was he never held up to his end of the bargain. Every time I bargained, I gave a little piece of myself away, tucked a little piece of hope deeper, or buried one of my dreams. I needed to change my bargaining ways. I felt as though he would say whatever he thought I wanted him to say, just to get past the conversation.

Lee pleaded with me about doing a separation or not getting a divorce. Just have affairs, stay married, and keep our life the same, as usual.

Excuse me? How fucking convenient!

One way or another, I was going to look like shit. I can do that on my own. (*If this was a TV show, the water cooler crowd would be fighting over who was more messed up!*)

I think for the first time in my life I said, "No, this is it."

Truth seared like hot swords through his brain. Eventually he broke down. I moved to comfort him, holding him tightly, kissing his hair, stoking his back. He gripped onto me, sobbing into my chest. He said, "Please don't leave, I'll do anything. Don't do this to Tasha."

I broke down crying, too. I ached that I was putting him through this misery. I looked to God and the universe for strength, but continued to sob into Lee's hair, rocking us back and forth to dull the pain.

All I could say to him was, "What do I teach her if I stay?"

I did tell him that Oscar was coming to visit in a couple weeks and that I would be out of the house within a couple days. I said we needed to tell Tasha, together. All the research I had done on it said that it was best to tell kids directly beforehand, and to be age-appropriate honest. We agreed to tell her about what was happening and not to stretch it out, so she wouldn't have to wait until it happened.

The next morning, Tasha was finishing her breakfast of pancakes with jam and fruit. Lee walked in, and we both took a deep breath. Tasha sensed that something was up. As if he was tattletaling, Lee said, "Tasha, Mom has something to tell you."

I explained to Tasha as soothingly as possible, "Daddy and I both love you so much, and we love being a family and always will be, but Daddy and I have a problem being married, and those are two different things."

Tasha looked confused and turned to Lee for help; he had none. Her eyes swelled with tears and her face turned red just as her tears burst. She stood up, ready to run, "I don't want to be a divorced kid, you're ruining my life!" Then she ran into Lee's arms. Lee looked desperately at me. I began to tear, but embraced them both, and we cried together.

I moved out the next day.

Lee - 3

From the moment I saw Tasha come out of Jules, I fell in love with this precious little girl. I spent lots of time with Tasha, and almost everyone thought I was the world's greatest dad. Many women wished that their husband would be a dad like I was.

I wanted to make it easier on Jules, so I would take Tasha with me for the day on bike rides, or let her drive, sitting on my lap...just special things a daddy does with his girl. I'd bring her to my office and show her off to all the people there. I'd bring her to visit all my family, take her fishing off the dock at the cabin... she was my little pal. She liked doing the things I liked to do and we loved being together. I don't think I knew fatherhood would be so special for me. I didn't really think about what it would do for my marriage.

I always felt there was jealousy from Julie over the relationship between Tasha and myself. I think a lot of it has to do with the hard childhood that she had, and the fact that she never felt she got the attention she wanted or needed. I could see that Julie wanted to be the one who was tickled or got a lot of attention. It was very hard to balance my time with both. I don't think I would act any differently with Tasha than I did. *I would definitely act differently with Julie.* I know that our problems go way back before Tasha was born, but I know that my relationship with Tasha was a factor in our splitting up.

Julie is the kind of person who likes to have change, and change used to drive me crazy. Julie had numerous different types of jobs. She couldn't stick to one thing, whether it be singing telegrams, or selling real estate, or working in a Jewish camp office as the business manager. In my opinion, she was trying to make me happy, but that's not who Julie was. She was too free a spirit to work in an accounting firm, although she tried and did well at it. If it wasn't something that she loved to do, she'd change, and move on to the next interest or job.

Even to this day, I laugh at how she changes her furniture around. There is nothing wrong with it—it's Julie's way of thinking, her way of living. We have our differences. I am into consistency and having a comfort zone. I am most comfortable when things are orderly, but I have to admit, I used to laugh at my dad or my brother for their idiosyncrasies. Now, I see some of them in my own traits.

We've all got those characteristics. I always wanted to have a large closet, so that I would be able to put all my clothes in neatly, by color, size, and style. It's a little superficial, but...*recently, I remodeled. Built-ins!!*

When Julie first asked me to see a psychic, I said, as usual, "No." I thought, *'craziness.'* Today, I'd call it "*adventurous.*" I didn't think it could help us in any way. I felt it was a stretch to see someone who was not educated in helping people with marital problems. Of course, I didn't really think we needed to see anybody. After Julie convinced me to go see one particular psychic, and we each had individual sessions, I was blown away by what the psychic said to me and us, and how accurate she was in defining our relationship. We then went to a few different counselors and therapists for help. In my opinion, they were the ones who seemed to need the help.

At the last therapist, when I finally said those fatal words about our sex life, Julie wasn't as much mad as she was relieved--She wasn't crazy. I called our sex life a 'marital obligation.' Couldn't really back out of those words in front of the therapist.

Obviously, neither avenue worked for me very well. Each of us were in a mental state where we were looking for something to grab hold of and say, "See, I told you." I hear that in a lot of married couple's conversations.

It was a subject that was very tough. I used to tell Julie that 80%, maybe 90% of our marriage was perfect (and, in my opinion, it really was great.) I think when you make a commitment for life, though, it has to be 100%. Sure, you're going to have arguments, disagreements, and have to make compromises at times. It takes a lot of energy for the first 80% of a marriage because that's a friendship, that's what bonds, that's what family is. That's where foundations are formed, but to make it really work, make it ideal, it takes 100%.

It was definitely hard to be 100% honest with friends. How could I tell them I was having sexual problems, I couldn't perform, I wasn't turned on by her, or I didn't have the energy? They would look at me, like... "What, are you nuts? Look at your wife! Are you absolutely crazy?"

Yeah, I just couldn't see myself having an open discussion about this.

When we spoke about when and if we would ever get divorced,

I discussed this almost as a martyr. I only talked about it to feel sorry for myself; in no way did I ever truly believe that we would get divorced. We were such good friends, confidants and more. Obviously not real good lovers, but that was one thing I never thought would split us up. Our discussions were serious for Julie, but not for me.

I believed that we would stay married forever and that these discussions were merely a tactic she used to try and wake me up, which I would do for a time; but I would always fall back asleep. I absolutely never had a clue Julie was having any kind of extramarital affairs. I was oblivious. The first time I actually knew Julie had an affair was when a letter came from someone who wanted to lash out at her. I actually read it first and then gave it to Julie.

Julie wanted to talk about it. I was in total denial. I brushed it aside, blocked it out as I had done with so many things in my life. I remember specifically saying, "Don't worry about it Jules, I know that she is just trying to cause friction between us, and I know that she did it out of spite and anger." Deep inside, I felt hurt and disgust, but on the outside I just couldn't look at it the way the letter should have affected me. Still, it hurt.

Julie wanted it to be an opportunity for us to have open discussions, as if this was a 2 x 4 to hit me over the head. It could have been a real turning point. There were many times I remember telling Jules, "You know, if you're not getting it from me, go out and find it somewhere else." So how could I really get upset with her?

I never really thought that she would go somewhere else, though, because our marriage was so great. There was just no way in the world that she would want to lose a man like me, because I was such a good guy. *I was such a good guy externally, but internally I wasn't that great of a husband. I wasn't that great of a companion to her.*

Julie having an affair, it wasn't just her fault. I made her go look somewhere else. I didn't give her a reason to stay in our bedroom.

There were some wonderful times in our marriage, as well. I remember the night in Vegas when we renewed our vows. It was very romantic--but typical Lee Liberman—I screwed up. Many things I said made no sense. I used to get very, very angry when I was married, maybe because I didn't have a way out...of what?

I'm not sure, but I did feel trapped between my Dad and Julie, often. The problem was, then, where did what I wanted fit in to what they wanted of me?

Sometimes I have a hard time going back to these memories, because it's not a person I like to see. I would tell Julie what she wanted to hear just to calm us down and move us on until everything blew up again.

Today I'm not as angry at her, at family, at life in general. You know, I never put two and two together that she was actually cleaning and moving, and making sure that the house was going to be left perfectly for me when she did actually move out. I wouldn't have to do much to it. Even though we said we would give it a six-month window, even with the time frames we gave each other, I was asleep. I would say, "Go have an affair. But always come back to me."

When I first heard that Julie wanted a divorce I was absolutely shocked. Before I left for Orlando that week, Julie had just come back from the Cayman Islands with a girlfriend. We only had one night at home together. That night we had sex, but like most nights, it was not that wonderful for either of us. On that particular night, there was something different about our sex. A smell that had never been there in the past. I chalked it up to our dysfunctional sex life and left the next morning without another thought about it.

My flight home was scheduled to leave late in the afternoon. Usually, if there was an earlier flight, I would try to get on it and arrive home earlier. Julie was persistent in telling me to stay longer, enjoy the sun for the day, "lie around the pool and just relax." I thought, *how nice that she appreciates how hard I work.*

We had not seen each other much in the last few weeks, but my wife knew I needed some time for myself. Still, I wanted to get back and be with her and Tasha. I did buy a bathing suit at the hotel gift shop and laid by the pool, trying to read a magazine and relax. Soaking in the sun and having some peace and quiet was great, but I could not contain myself for long. I was itching to get home. It seemed like a waste of time to stay in Orlando. Because of my late flight, I wouldn't be able to see Tasha until the next morning.

When I arrived in Minneapolis that evening, Julie—late as usual, picked me up at the airport. I always tried to look good for her when I returned from a business trip. I was dressed in my 'Miami Vice' outfit, black-lined sport coat, t-shirt, white pants and black shoes. Julie pulled up but didn't get out of the car, I realized I was riding shotgun. I put my suitcase in the back and got in. She was busy writing something in her date book. We gave each other a sixteen-years-married kiss, hello.

On the drive back to our house, I told her how good it felt to be home, and how great she looked. We talked about what was going on in Minneapolis, how her family was, what Tasha was doing, things about friends—small talk we had exchanged a hundred times before.

There was absolutely no indication of what was about to unfold.

When I arrived at home, it looked perfect. Julie's friends used to joke that the house always looked like no one lived there when I was in town. When I wasn't in town, it was a whole other story. I knew Julie had put the time and energy into making it nice for me. I went into Tasha's bedroom and gave her a kiss, then played with our dog, Frankie Boy, for a while. After I unpacked, I met Julie out on the deck for a smoke.

The moon was out, and it was an absolutely beautiful night. The lawn service had been there during the day. The lawn was mowed and I could see the lines that the mower made. That night, the pool was gleaming with the reflection of the moon on it; everything was perfect, I thought. Absolutely perfect.

As we were standing on the deck smoking, Julie said she had something to tell me, but she did not know how, so she had put it down on paper. Even at this point, I hadn't a clue about what was going on. Everything seemed so normal, and then I read her letter.

What the hell did I just read?!

I thought it was an "I want a divorce letter," but I knew it couldn't be. I knew this could not be happening to me. To us. We got along so great.

I wanted to vomit. Julie looked so fragile and scared. I kept thinking, *we have a perfect life!*

I knew we had sexual problems, I knew we had talked about doing something about it, but in general our life was great. I knew I'd made lots of promises I might not have kept. I knew many things I had said I would change, I hadn't. I knew I was somewhat anal when it came to a few things, okay, maybe more than a few things. I knew that I made Julie walk on eggshells and there were numerous other things that I did that drove her insane, but come on, divorce?!

There were so many marriages weaker than ours. I could not believe that this was actually happening. What should I tell Tasha? "Your mom wants to divorce me; she doesn't love your daddy anymore?"

I stood up and went to where Julie was sitting. I started crying and screaming for help. "Help me understand where this came from?" I said, "How dare you do this to me, how could you, after so many years of great times? We had some bad times too, but they were mostly good. How could you want to give this up? "

I reminded her that I had provided a wonderful life for us. Financially, I was doing well. I never kept her from doing what she wanted to do. I never cheated on her once, rarely even looked the other way. I always wanted to be with her as much as possible to show her that I loved her, and wanted to be with her, just not socially.

You can talk, you can discuss, you can even say to yourself, "It's going to happen," but, when it does, you are in disbelief--or at least I was, for sure. I sat that evening in the perfect moonlight, watching my perfect life..., watching it dissolve around me.

Julie's letter to Lee:

My Dearest Boo,

Where do I begin? I'm not sure where to start since we've been going along as though these six months I gave myself never happened or existed. We just kept going without taking inventory, but my vacation allowed me to stop long enough to do just that. I want to talk but don't know how to bring it up.

Leeor, you know I love you, have always, always will.

I thought I could convince myself that I should be grateful to have such a wonderful man as my husband and father to my child. You really are and I'm grateful to have you in my life and Tasha is so lucky to have a dad like you.

You have broken the mold and given her so much more then either of us had. You have grown as a being who sees life beyond the trivial everyday things.

You know that one of my issues in life is integrity. It surfaces just when I think I've got it covered. It isn't just integrity to you or our marriage, it is to me, to Tasha and my life. I've learned there are so many levels of integrity, many of them conflicting with others. I realize that especially with you, this issue has resurfaced over and over again these past years, simply because we have a history we cannot escape or move forward from together. It has worked and served us both well for many years, nurturing each other to grow into higher selves, but like a womb that eventually is too small for the growth, it's time for us--at least for me and I believe yourself as well--to be born into a new life.

I do love you and don't want to hurt you any more then you do me. But at a <u>very deep</u> level, we are crushing each other's ability to move to the next level.

When you get beyond the shock, and into your own life and what you decide to do with it, I think you will realize that it is partially me keeping you back from doing what's true to you.

I have felt very alone in much of my life. I'm <u>not</u> blaming you. I just need to express my true self freely and with integrity to myself--which is in conflict with having integrity to you and our marriage.

I have decided to move on. I know there will be much pain for many people, especially Tasha, you, and me. It won't be easy and there will be grieving of a life lost. But there will also be much opportunity, even if you don't see that now. I believe it's best for all of us and what's next is deciding how to do it. We have discussed options before, but we really must consider Tasha first.

I'm sorry. I do love you. And I do believe that this is for the best.

Love always, J

Tasha - 3

My DaD is the bast
he tichis me las of
sporst my fevrit sporst
is sacr. He hlpe weth
my homework. I hope
my mom never brak
up weth my DaD.

TASHA

M.N

CHAPTER 3 DISCUSSION

Recognizing Our "Perfect Life" Expectations

What happens when we attain our goal of the "Perfect Life" and it's not perfect? What does one do when love is not enough to keep a marriage alive and working? How did we not know it would be so hard? Why is our marriage the only one out there that doesn't work? Just what are we willing to do and not do now that we are here? What did our vows mean? Or the other's vows, for that matter?

There are those of us who are sensual beings. That doesn't mean it's about having sex all the time, but that--sensuality, on all levels of physical, mental, emotional, and spiritual--are an integral part of the functioning of the whole being. We are alive souls embodied on the physical plane to manifest life. I believe, all souls (taking this challenge of "life embodied") will suffer and rejoice, and will experience pain and pleasure. To me, they are all things of life to experience if we are to really live life; not just survive it, but LIVE it. To really be courageous, we must know, name and face our fears.

It's accepted that most marriages are based on a monogamous relationship. Marriage, somehow in the last century, has been idealized to mean we have found our "one and only," and with that goes verbal, physical, mental, emotional and spiritual idolatry. However, is 'true love' correctly identified through possession of another? With each love song crooning about needing to belong to the other or wanting to forever hold onto this love, we are fed another dose of possessive love that is truly based on ego rather than on selflessness. Still, monogamy is the underlying principal in marriage. We believe that possessing another fulfills our needs. When that ownership is interrupted, suffering entails based on the fear of losing that possession we have named 'true love.' Even if we are not truly in love with our partner, we are betrayed when they find love in someone else's arms.

Once betrayal has entered a marriage on whatever level, there is usually a stage where an agreement is made to try to work things out to "Stay married for the sake of the kids," or because "Divorce doesn't happen in my family," or, maybe even "Let's try everything we can first, so we can say didn't just give up." We have needs that may conflict with one another, not only within the relationship, but within our selves. We may wish for both our marriage to work and to end within the same moment.

We might concede small or great allowances for the other in some ways, perhaps even taking some responsibility for the betrayal and what our own part was that escalated the situation to come to this. Therapy always helps, depending on the therapist, of course. But, that means we must face our selves and our own misguidances. Naming in our own self what we see in others is the hardest part of the learning curve of self-discovery. Others are simply the mirror of our own image that we do not yet recognize, allowing us to see a reflection we may not want to acknowledge. If we sweep them under the rug, they'll go away. Right?

We may have discovered what we don't want in life, but aren't sure what exactly we do want. New things have become important to us that were not until now. Middle age approaches, and the feeling of "this is it, now or never, do or die," becomes a fantasized theme. We may feel as though we have been asleep in our lives, simply going from moment to moment, rather than consciously living, wide-awake and seeing clearly rather than walking, dead to the world, in delusions built by fears.

But, perhaps, there are roadblocks of our fears that slap us back to our reality. *It's not so bad, it could be worse out there.* At least we know what we've got, and are not afraid of what we've got enough to leave it in exchange for the fear of the unknown. When "where we are" is more frightening than the "unknown" is, this is where most will finally move. Nevertheless, these actions may be based on fear, and may not be made with wisdom or compassion. Fear is the opposite of Love.

<u>Evocations:</u>

1. What happens if I'm not perfect? Or you're not who you say you are?
2. What happens if we do get "perfect" but our parameters change?
3. What happens if all the perfect plans fall through due to circumstances?
4. Do I look for what's right? Or do I look for what's wrong?
5. Do I have the wisdom to change what I can and let go of what I cannot change? Can I tell the difference?
6. How do I stand in my own power while trying to please another?
7. Do I use my sadness to beat myself/others up, or to assist growth?
8. What do our vows mean, exactly? Why are they important?

CHAPTER FOUR

In the Eye of the Storm, Living the Hurricane

Julie

On April 1st, 2000, I drove away from my 4, 000 square foot home that every corner had some piece of my life--every painting, every picture, every piece of furniture, every fabric that I had woven to make my life. All my stuff narrowed down into one car. A girlfriend of mine had just bought a house she wouldn't be moving into for a couple months. It was completely empty. I could hide there while I figured out what to do next.

It was so sad and exhilarating at the same time, filled with such loss and such hope. That day, we told our families and friends, mockingly, "No, it's not an April Fool's Day prank. This is it. We really are getting divorced."

In everyone's eyes, I had crazily left the perfect life. I was the one who moved out, to the horror of several family and friends. I was resolved in knowing that I needed to leave Lee. Yet, here was another man, coming on the 'toes' of my divorce before I had even touched the water with them.

Oscar came to visit, with practically all his belongings. He never left. Somehow, we decided that the best thing at the time was for him to stay. The scandal was set and locked. He was such an adventurer for showing up in another country; *how daring, brave, and courageous*, I thought. It didn't cross my mind that he would be running away from the life he '*left for me.*'

I looked at the new hole in the ceiling Oscar had made. I laughed and scanned the room with all of its destruction. The bathroom in front of me was ripped down to the studs. The kitchen wall was gone, and electrical wires hung from the ceiling. There was dust everywhere. Plastic covered the furniture but was disheveled. Boxes were everywhere and the TV was on CNN describing the latest hurricane, *Oscar.*

"Soon it will be our dream home, you'll see, I promise you. It'll be beautiful when I am through." Then he pulled me into him and began to salsa dance. I laughed as he swirled me around. I responded, "Promises, promises."

I finally ripped my life apart with the assistance of my newfound *love of my life.* I was not making rational decisions, although, when had I? I had become drugged in love, lust, and having a social life with a man--with those who chose to accept him in my life.

We were giddy in love. One night in our hotel room while on vacation, a howling storm raged outside. The lights flickered as we finished off the bottle of champagne. I was drunk. Oscar's fingers gently closed my eyes, and then, as seductive music played in the background, he fed me chocolates. He had me lick each of his fingers and I swooned as he worked his kisses around to the back my neck, so passionately that the world began to melt away. He had found a way to make me comply with whatever he asked.

He wanted to make a videotape of us making love. I reluctantly agreed with the understanding that we would erase it right away. I said, "Promise?" I looked at him wondering if I could trust him. He rushed to set up the camera before I changed my mind. The camera rolled as lightening struck and our lovemaking reeled into full force.

Afterwards, he saw that I looked troubled and distant. He tried to cheer me up. He lit candles, jumped on the bed, and said, "Come on movie star, let's see our creation." I was horrified, embarrassed and could barely watch.

My cell phone rang and Lee's voice screamed through the phone. Frankie, our beloved family dog had died in his arms. Lee, who had never ever let the dog lick anything or anyone because of the disgusting germs in his mouth, did his best to help Frankie breathe by giving him mouth-to mouth resuscitation during his last moments.

I crumbled; guilt surged through me for having been so far away and with another man. Oscar tried to comfort me, but I moved away. Oscar was noticeably irritated. He turned off the camera and silently put it away before he pulled the covers over himself. I turned away; this was my time with Lee.

After I hung up, I curled up in a ball and sobbed uncontrollably. Oscar removed the pillow from his head and tenderly said, "Frankie was a great dog."

That was the most heroic thing I had ever known Lee to do. He leapt out of his box of fear when the reality of Frankie's death was in front of him. *This was an example of the true character of the man I have loved over all of these years and through all of his fears.* His fears in his day-to-day life kept him gripped into a set of rules of thought and action that were not his true nature. I had witnessed his true nature, though his fears had done well to keep it hidden.

I returned home the next day. Lee and I struggled in keeping to our civilized plan for divorce with Oscar in the picture. One member of my family strongly urged Lee to take full custody of Tasha because of my madness with Oscar-- convinced it would be a correct retribution for me to pay. A couple relatives even told me I needed to be *publicly ostracized* by my family. I did my best to understand their own histories and how all this must have affected them, but it felt like being kicked in the gut when you're already down and bleeding. There were people at the time, in order to uphold their life's structure of how life is defined for them, who felt a need to convince us that our divorce must be hateful, and that it couldn't be anything but. In reality, many people were very supportive, but the squeaky wheel is the one that is heard loudest.

A church banner I passed daily, that changed weekly, always seemed to be speaking to me. (Ok, I'm a little crazy, but at the funniest times, it does say just what is needed.) At one point it read, *Friends are plenty in prosperity, but prove themselves in adversity.* I found out I had many dear friends that year. I am ever grateful for them.

Lee was shaky and angry the moment he brought up taking full custody. The energy he emitted was so strongly against me. I was shocked. My heart felt stabbed. I pulled at my hair and silently screamed, insanity hit. My beloved boy had just died and I was losing my daughter now, too! I began to pace and began to feel both manic and paralyzed at the same time before registering deep sadness.

"Maybe she would be better without me as her mother. Maybe it would be easier on everyone if I just disappeared." I started to walk to my car— to vanish.

Lee urgently said, "She needs you in her life no matter what anyone says." He grabbed me and I melted into him sobbing, silently. I was doing my best with Tasha over the several years but it was a struggle to be a good parent every day of my life. I had so much to learn. If I didn't teach her about being truthful to herself, than how could she ever be truthful with others? I may have seemed crazy to expose her to such 'wretched' truths, but in reality, she had watched much worse on TV. I did my best to teach her to be truthful, even when you are afraid of what others will think, say, or do.

When I look back at that time, I kept asking God what to do. I knew I was 'doing wrong' and yet, I kept getting the message that it is not the act that God judges, but how it is done. I was so stripped of any masks I had worn in my life; there was nothing left but the raw truth.

I hadn't introduced Tasha to Oscar in the first couple of weeks thinking that it was just a vacation. It was really difficult managing it. Oscar had many needs for my time, but he loved me and was willing to take these risks with me. We decided that he would stay and we would see how it went for the summer, if we could make a long-term relationship work, I determined that I needed to tell Tasha the truth.

I needed to create a relationship with her outside of Lee's house. This meant that she would start coming to my home, which was not even a home, yet. I was still at my girlfriend's house, with Oscar. Before she moved in with all her furniture, I had a folding lawn chair in my living room as a couch and a cardboard table. I had no lamps so I put up Christmas lights up in every room, even though it was April. Blue lights, different colored lights, white lights all around the house. I wasn't allowed to put them up for seventeen years because they're called Christmas lights even though they're just lights, so it was the first thing I did. It had such a warm glow to it, such a surreal feeling.

At that point, I had to figure out how to tell my almost 8-yr-old girl that I'm living with another man. Can she understand that? What it means? Surely, adults who understand what it meant thought I shouldn't tell her, that it was wrong of me to introduce him to her. But, I was living with this man. How can I live that lie? How could I even try to hide it? How can I have any integrity to myself if I don't own my own actions? How could I teach Tasha to own her individual actions? It was already an issue and struggle.

Kids are resilient. Kids can take things. It's us adults that have all the head-trips. We oblige them on the children. Tasha took my telling her about Oscar much better than I expected, than anyone expected, really. To her, a child, Oscar was just another person. It wasn't about a man and a woman, but she understood that I had a special relationship with him. They would speak Spanish together. They had their little secrets between them. She did adore him; she did come to love him.

Many people, including Lee, had not yet met Oscar by the time Tasha had. In their minds, it was beyond comprehension that Tasha should be exposed to this monstrous relationship, or that I could sincerely love both men.

Was I the first in history to have this problem?

After a painful phone call I had with Lee, Oscar was furious, "Love you Boo? That's how you speak to your ex-husband when you are in bed with me?" He was right. It was absurd. Nevertheless, I had always called him Boo, and I did love him, whether we fought or not, married or not—*which we still were!*

My love for Oscar did not diminish my love for Lee. This, too, seemed unfathomable to others. It was unfathomable to me, how much I could hurt the people I loved.

Still, Lee and I spoke every day. That was something that drove Oscar, and everybody else, crazy. Oscar had cut out so many people in his life that he had loved, and that had loved him, that he didn't understand the concept of what Lee and I were trying to do in our divorce. Not many did understand. Although, there were many who thought we were doing a good job for Tasha's well-being, as much as we could. Her school counselor and teachers were keeping us abreast of how she was doing. The counselor put together a divorce class for the five children in Tasha's class who were going through their own familial shifts. It seemed to really help her feel not so abnormal. She knew she had it better than some other kids whose parents acted as if they hated each other and used the kids to fight between them.

So, it was difficult, especially when Tasha had asked Oscar to come to her school concert. Lee thought it was me who invited Oscar to the concert.

Lee would ping pong between being really incredibly the Buddha, to being a child that does not think about his words. Before the concert, he said, "If you dare to show up with him at our daughter's school..." and then thirty minutes later waves at us from the front row that he's saved us two seats next to him.

WHOA!

Was that the consequence of my dare? Because, let me tell you, it sucked. I walked down the aisle, reminding myself to breathe. *Just breathe...*

This was quite the public turning point--Tasha's school concert. The auditorium was full of people. Lee, Oscar and I sat in the front row, me between them. When Tasha came out on stage, all that mattered was that she saw me sitting between the two of them and she smiled. The pride she had, showing her friends that we were all there. She sang so beautifully. It was such an alive moment for all of us. With every feeling of everything that was going on, it was a bittersweet moment in life. *Trust me, I heard the group of school moms "tisk-tisking" me, but I chose to keep my head up.*

I should have just disappeared... Maybe that would have been easiest on everyone. It certainly would have been easier on me. Every grocery store I walked into, every mall, every movie, every restaurant, every school function, every everything that I walked into during this time of my scandalous affair, my divorce was right in front of me. I knew so many people. I could not go anywhere without it being in my face. I'm not a person who was taught that being confrontational was good. I always let people confront me, but I was really only good at it when it was on someone else's behalf. Then, there are people who are not afraid to say whatever they want to say. As I was stretching myself in this area, I must have opened a Pandora's Box. Sometimes, things just popped out, as if someone was inside of me that was defending me. That voice would say exactly what was needed to shut the other up and, put them in their place--out of my face. *It worked!*

Some of the cruel things I would reply when I felt attacked even took me aback. Even if what I said was true, I am embarrassed to have stooped that low. Yet, there is a Jewish saying that goes, "If I am not for myself, who will be?" It gave me strength and the power to talk back to the offensive attacks. My favorite, admittedly, was the one who threw judgment on my affair and its publicity. I responded, "So yours, that you think are secret, are okay, then?" That conversation ended quickly.

I struggle with 'not' being proud of that, and being VERY proud of that newly acquired skill to stand up for myself… but it was a tool that I had not learned how to use with finesse, so sometimes, I inflicted great gouges with a force that surprised all who encountered it, myself included. But I was not going to throw the tool away. I was going to learn how to wield it with strength, conviction, compassion and mercy. This newfound 'blade' of speaking the truth would not only clear my garden and fields of gnarly and decayed roots from past plantings, but it would tend and harvest the new garden, as well.

Another inevitable circumstance associated with divorce is the difficulty involved in the children's home life, where they stay and when. Since I had always been in charge of Tasha's care, for the most part, the fact that I left the house rather than make Lee leave it, was to save them both the added suffering on his psyche, and therefore hers. It was hard enough without me there. Having a new home altogether, is an entirely added challenge of its own on top of that. Tasha and I were more resilient to change. However, I needed to continue to teach her to be resilient to life's changes.

Predictably, Tasha really did not like coming to the new house. She enjoyed Oscar and of course spending time with us, but she did not like leaving Dad alone. She did not like having to leave him to come be with me. Her bedroom was not as nice. The pool was not as nice—we bought a mock up from Target. Just about nothing was as nice as at Dad's house. She wanted to be loving, but there was still anger underneath a lot of what she would say or do or behave like with me. The struggle of getting her to come stay with me was getting harder.

It had been two months since Frankie, our dog, had died… just a couple months after I had moved out. It was the worst timing in the world to get a dog, what with the house being ripped apart and all, but Oscar and I agreed. We brought Tasha with us. We let her pick out which one she wanted. She was finally happy to come to the house to play with the new dog, to have a puppy to sleep with. They were so cute together.

All the while, Lee was doing his best to be supportive of me knowing that I looked like an adulterer to the entire family and community, but he could not come clean about his piece about how he was unwilling to work on our marriage. His guilt consumed him and yet I was the only person he could talk to about it. He knew my love was still true, yet bruised. Still, he continued to support me in many ways, even though I continued a relationship with Oscar, openly.

For years before we ever divorced, we had frequently spoken about how we would do it. We were determined not to go to court other than to get that last judge's signature. I think there was concern from his business that I would try to take money from it. Even though, legally, I could have taken half of his share, I felt we had enough between us in our holdings for me to get started on my own. I was only 36, intelligent and ready to take care of myself.

We wrote down everything that we could think of on a piece of paper: insurance, bonds, and art, whatever... We totaled it up and began to decide what we each would keep. The stocks we had equaled the equity in the house, so he kept the house and I kept the stocks. At that point, the market was doing quite bullish and I thought I'd be just fine. A couple items we both wanted... so we figured out how to get another copy of a painting, and he made me copies of all our home movies... We figured it out... 'Things' just didn't matter to me so much. I would acquire them again in my life... It's the memories I didn't want to lose.

Oscar and I soon had many difficult situations, as our love affair quickly became the real life drama of day-to-day living. I sat at my computer, eyes glazed over with piles of bills, files, and projects and photos and books and magazines overflowing from every inch. Oscar walked in with two drinks. I said, "No thanks, I've got a bunch of work to do and I don't even know where to start. Also, I'm looking at the bills, and honey; I hope that money was transferred into your account. I'm short what you owe me."

I had figured it to be close to $5,000. Oscar sifted through the desk, found his checkbook and started to write a check. With masterful distraction, he told me that he had finally spoken to his long lost son that afternoon. I was so happy for him. I dropped everything and turned to him lovingly, wanting to know what he had said.

He told me how he had called, and his ex-wife allowed him to talk to his son. We cried together and he thanked me for encouraging him to finally get back in touch with them. He pulled me into him, kissing me wildly. I melted. I hadn't even noticed that he had slipped his checkbook back into its place.

I get pregnant. The timing is horrible...This time I was worse off than an unwed mother. I was married, but living with my *Latin* lover.

Then there was Tasha, who was so afraid of me leaving to start another family... I decided not to have this baby. I was not ready to be locked into something that might not last.

Oscar was horrified and hurt by my decision, yet fluctuated with it being the only 'right' thing to do. Afterwards, he fought with me and told me to get out of the house. I reminded him he was in my house. He ended up leaving.

I felt the most liberated I had ever been, having stood up for myself to him in his emotional tirade against me. He came back on his knees, begging for my forgiveness and for me to take him back. I held my ground, but I did take him to the airport first thing the next morning. I gave him $1,500 to get by on until he could figure things out, and then asked him about the sex tape he told me he would erase long ago. He told me that it was still in the cupboard. He frowned at me that I would even question him about something like that. I returned home to find the tape and even more money missing.

I went into a humiliated rage, sinking lower into hell than I'd already been. How could I have been so taken by this person? He really started to show signs of mental illness. He called me over and over and over again. He confessed. He pleaded and cried. He tried to make amends by saying that he hadn't tried to hurt me; he just loved me so much that he wanted the tape to remember how we loved one another. That wasn't doing the trick. I already let myself be tricked.

I was so angry.

He finally wasn't there everyday so I was able to step back and try to get a clear picture of why I was so in love with this man. I was really ready to let him go, and just be done with this wretched chapter in my life.

But, no, not me. I still clung to the idea that maybe love could really conquer all the problems… About a week later, I heard from him. His voice sounded different. It was the voice of the man I had met; instead of the pathetic, whimpering man who had left. His voice was strong and full of purpose. He was angry with me. I thought, hmmm, *this is interesting*.

We spoke and he told me about how he almost died saving a man's life aboard the ship. A bad storm had come. He had already gotten out of the water and removed all his gear, when one of his treasure hunting buddies was trying to get out of the water and hit his head on the ladder as a big wave came and threw him off the boat. Oscar watched this happen. His shipmate was being tossed around and Oscar knew he had passed out. Oscar dove back into the water and rescued him. He brought the man to the others who pulled him out of the water.

As that was happening, Oscar was thrown against the ship, also. He was sucked under water with that last wave. He had been so depressed that he thought, *this is it, this is my time, this is when I get to die*. He allowed himself to go under. But, as he was sinking, something sparked. Something made him angry.

He told me he thought, *I'm not going to end my life because of her. I'm not going to be wasting my life away because she is not having me there with her. I have dreams and I'm going to live.* Therefore, as retaliation against me representing his death, he pulled himself out of the water because he was going to live. He was going to survive and thrive, with me or without me.

In that instant, he chose to re-create his life, with a fresh slate. He was reborn in that moment when he was about to die. The strength was back in his voice, the determination, and the absolute resolve that his life was his own whether I joined him or not. Yes, he'd love to share his life with me, but no, he is not going to die because I'm not there.

That, to me, was a turning point. I was willing to look at him again, finally able to talk to him again. He didn't need to lie anymore, he said. He sent me back the tape and said not to worry, *there were no copies.*

Looking back, I don't know what would be the trigger in his head for the storyteller in him to come out, but I really believe that one of his personas loved me so deeply that he would say anything to be able to have another day with me. (I know that must sound entirely egotistical, but the question is, then, what in the world motivated him to lie to me all those times. Is it just the fact that once you start, you can't stop—like a drug?)

I offered, again, what I had said to him six months earlier. *Let's be loving, let's have a relationship, but let's not change our lives this moment. Let's just see how it goes. Let's visit one another once a month. Let's enjoy time together without it being about 'are we getting married or aren't we getting married.'* I did miss him. I did miss having a loving relationship.

Lee had been very kind to me during the month Oscar was first gone. I could see that wasn't going to go anywhere other than us being able to be very kind and supportive to each other. It seemed to me that he hadn't really changed. He hadn't really grown. He was still lying to himself, to me, and to others about what was going on in our marriage, and in our divorce. But I loved being with him still.

At that point in my life, through all my studies of healing modalities, I was most thankful to have begun a deeper Yoga practice. It was definitely having an impact on my ability to stay balanced under duress, and be more flexible in my thoughts, more open in my heart. Somehow, the universe brought together the little pieces that had blown apart from the hurricane Oscar had whipped into our lives. Everything, but nothing, had seemed to change. I finished remodeling the house. When Oscar did return for a visit, he was simultaneously pleased that it was done, and hurt that it was done without him. *I never knew what to expect.*

Lee - 4

I remember the first time I found out about Oscar. Julie said that it was a fling, but exactly what she needed to go ahead and move on with her life, and out of our home. Although I was pissed, I do not know what made me *not* get mad at her. It was ironic that with all the pain that I was feeling at the time, I was still trying to protect Julie and, of course, our daughter, from all that would be said about Julie. *Not me, of course, people will blame her. I was the good guy.*

I was also hurt, angry, jealous, and many more feelings that I had to go through, in my own way. During our split and the coming of Oscar there were, I'm sure, plenty of rumors and gossiping around town. It did affect me quite a bit. One of the hardest things that I had to go through was the '*What do people think of me?*' stage. I did go see a therapist for a little while after our divorce, but I thought it was absolutely a waste of time and money. All the right questions were being asked, so I gave it a shot. But, it wasn't what I was looking for. This therapist tried to get things out of me that really were not inside of me. I cancelled the next meeting.

The first night that Julie wasn't in my bed, well obviously, it was kind of like the same as when 'no one is there.' Actually, you know what? That's something that Julie might say, "*Would it make a difference whether* **I'm** *here or not here, because you don't want* **me**."

It was definitely difficult whether she was next to me or she was not next to me. I used to love holding and hugging, spooning and just a nice warm body next to mine, which I still do miss to this day. Sexually or not sexually, having her next to me was always nice, you know? A husband and wife type of deal. I never ever once thought I was going to come home to see the missing pieces of the home that we had put together over many years. It was very difficult for me and I'm sure it was a difficult time for Tasha, as well.

Tasha had her first few days at Julie's. I was actually terrified to stay in the big old house by myself. It was kind of hard the first couple of nights when nobody was here because I could hear the creaks and the cracks... all that kind of stuff you don't notice if someone else is there. I don't know if it was hard because they weren't there, or because I was just a chicken shit.

I was always afraid of the dark. I never liked going downstairs at night. I'd always make Julie go down, and I'd follow six or seven steps behind in case I had to run away quick. All of the sudden, I had to do it by myself, all alone, well, with my baseball bat. Sometimes, I'd even take the flashlight so I could see where the light switch was.

The first things I did when Tasha moved to Julie's was to make her bed, hang up her clothes and straighten her closet, clean the kitchen drawers, put tape and scissors where they belonged... I just straightened and cleaned everything the way I wanted it. I wasn't ready to go out into the world. I wanted to stay home and get things done. I wanted things done the way Julie never did them in 17 years, like the silverware drawer, stacked perfectly instead of tossed in at random. I put all the pens facing the right way, stuff I enjoyed... coffee cups laid on the shelf by color code and handle to the correct degreed angle. I was on a strong cleansing mode... closet after closet after closet...that house has a lot of closets and even more drawers... gorgeous, clean drawers.

I had no social life at all. I was in a very hibernated state, very little family interaction except for at the office. I wasn't ready to be out there yet, tagged as divorced. It just didn't feel right. I just didn't feel like being looked at, whispered about, even though Julie and I talked about stepping up and into those awkward moments..., it was a gradual movement.

To get myself out, I shopped. I spent money on the most ridiculous things you or I could ever imagine. I suddenly became a collector of knick-knacks... everything began to multiply, from spices in cute little bottles, oils in glass or mosaic holders. I changed all the photo frames in the house to match each other. Then, I re-did all the photo albums. Julie always had different styles thrown together. These were the silly things that kept me happy. I just wanted the house clean.

I remember the first great day I had at my office, the first real excellent day I had had in many since Jules had left. I arrived home, and when I got to the driveway, I opened the garage, pulled in and realized what a thrill it was for me to have this huge garage to myself. We used to have a really small garage. Before Julie moved out, she remodeled and made it big enough for both of us to comfortably park in it. Before that, I had to drive up backwards if I wanted to open my car door enough to squeeze out of it.

Well, at the end of that first wonderful day, I saw an empty, clean garage, I was so excited about it that I pulled in and parked at an angle...diagonally across the garage! I remember opening the car door all the way, as far as it would open. I just sat there looking at it. It was such a thrill, a little happy moment in my garage. It just gave that day a magnificent finish.

Then, I walked into an empty house. It was an instant bummer. I shut down the minute I walked into what felt like a mausoleum of my life. But I tended it like a butler of a castle. I would go out and pick up dog poop after each time so it wouldn't ruin my lawn... loved my lawn... *Still do.* When Tasha came home, I told her to take her shoes off. She said, *like Julie would,* "Dad, we live here. We don't need to take our shoes off."

"Well," I replied, "You don't have to destroy things to enjoy them. One day when you grow up and spend money for the cleaning lady, we can talk."

With my house being so straight, to keep myself busy, I helped Jules. I re-arranged her garage... It's funny to me that there was always so much cleaning and arranging to do at her house... always such a mess...

Believe it or not, after the first three or four weeks of Julie and I being separated and heading into divorce, people that I've never heard of called. They were usually friends of my mom, trying to hook me up with every single Jewish divorced woman with two or three kids in the Twin Cities area. I would always say, "No."

The phone calls were ridiculous. I mean, I'd come home from work and there would two or three messages. It was absolutely absurd. It was a major turn off. I had been married for seventeen years and now, I needed time to evaluate myself. The bed was not even cold yet. The house still had her smell in it. The last thing that I wanted to do was start dating right away. I was also very protective, sometimes too much, of Tasha.

I had been on a few dates. There seemed to be a demand for Jewish divorcees. It was all right to go out on a quick note, or have a quick phone call; but it had to be under my terms. There are people that are just looking for companionship. Some are looking to hook up with you so you can take care of them and their kids. At that point, there was nobody I wanted to take care of more than just myself, and my daughter.

The first time I met Oscar was at Tasha's recital. I remember I told Jules that I would be sitting on the right. I told her, "If you walk in, do not stand on the right. Do not sit in the same section as I am. Sit away from me."

As usual, I got there very early and when I walked in and saw all these people, all the families together, I said, "Screw this, I'm sitting up front and I'm going to save two seats for Julie and Oscar." The auditorium was completely full and I kept turning my head every two or three seconds in case she had come in and sat on the left in the back. I wanted her to sit up front with me, even with Oscar.

Julie and Oscar walked in right before show time; our eyes met and I put my hand up and said, "Come on down this way." It caught her so off guard that she didn't have an option. She sat next to me and gave me a little kiss on the cheek and I gave her one. Oscar and I shook hands. Julie sat between us, nervous as hell.

When Tasha walked out on stage and saw all three of us in the front row, she had an absolute shocked look, which immediately turned into this beaming happy face. She had this smile on that you just can't describe; it made me cry. After the recital, I stood up, shook hands with Oscar again. Jules said, "What the hell happened to you? But, thank you..."

In a sense, it was the first time I actually behaved as a stronger person. With thanks to Julie, I was able to go through the awkward moments (*and there were many,*) with a sense of determination to show people, and myself, that whatever was thought, or whatever was said, I was going to make it through this stronger and as a better person for my family and myself. I would say, "To badmouth either one of us in this situation, does no good."

I also knew that I had put Julie in that situation. As angry, upset, and disappointed as I was, I knew I was part of the reason why he came up here. I felt terrible for Julie because I felt she also needed some time for herself and should not be in another relationship right away. There were so many emotions, so many family interferences going on, and of course, we needed to take care of our sweet little eight-year-old daughter.

I was still very worried about the label of divorce hanging over my head. It was a small community and now that everybody knew that there was another man in Julie's life, of course, they were going to fault her. People were just not able to understand that it was also me that was a part of the issue. It was a hard summer.

Only ten weeks after Julie moved out, our twelve-year-old

family Springer Spaniel had a seizure when Julie and Oscar were on a trip. I called the emergency vet. I did try to resuscitate him before his body shuddered and he died in my arms.

When I finally got a hold of Julie, she was consumed with grief, feeling as if she had abandoned him, that she had left without even saying good-bye. I assured her that she was the best mom a dog could ever have. I never let him kiss me. I was the fricking freak.

Julie wouldn't allow it. She was even stronger when telling me that I was the one that gave Frankie his last breath and that he knew how much I loved him. We both cried and screamed in pain at this last piece of our life together that had now been ripped away from us.

A couple of Julie's family members, because of Oscar, because of Julie's adulterer ways, pushed me to take full custody of Tasha. It never entered my mind that I wanted to have sole custody of her. A couple times, though, I did bring it up with Jules. They swayed me when I was weak. You know, telling me that Julie was 'not fit' and didn't deserve to be Tasha's mother. But, God, it wasn't just Julie. She wasn't a bad person.

Some of the things coming out of people's mouths were frightening. I could see where it really could take over people's psyche, like it did to mine on occasion... here and there... But, because I really didn't listen to Julie when we were married (in terms of what would have kept us together,) I knew if I was going to be the person I wanted to be in this divorce, I had to start listening to her.

What she did was probably the best thing for her life, and probably pretty scary, too. In the eyes of certain people, what she did was wrong and that meant she and her kind of lifestyle didn't deserve custody of her child. Many times I agreed, but, thank God, I was able to hear the one person that I still loved and still do love, Julie, the one that kept focusing on moving forward. At that time, I felt she was the only one giving me positive energy and reinforcement, versus the negative energy's reinforcement that I was getting left and right. That's the one thing we did have. We were able to communicate on many different levels.

I'm still so grateful that I was able to avoid going into this so-called, "Dark side" of divorce, but instead maintained what we had always gone for, to be equals when it came to the parenting of our child. Making decisions about her life, her well-being, her health, her schooling, and her extracurricular activities, all of that, we shared evenly and openly between the two of us.

I know that when Tasha was at Jules's house it was tough. It was very hard at the beginning. She loved and wanted to be with her mom, but, there was just more of a comfort level when she stayed in the home where she'd grown up. There were times when I left her with Jules and Oscar, that were very traumatic for her- for all of us, really. It was very hard on me, as well. It was heart wrenching knowing that my daughter was having a difficult time. Julie and Oscar bought a puppy to ease things for her. It did make it a little easier...

When Oscar left so abruptly, I was shocked but excited, sad for Julie and happy for Julie...It would give her time for herself to get her head together. For me, now there was a chance to get back together with her. But again, a great time for me to give her time by herself, for herself... and then see if things could start up again... slowly.

The idea of getting back together was just that, an idea. I don't think I really wanted it. I think, again, it was the idea of her coming back versus what I really wanted... I was on a high of living alone, doing whatever I wanted on the one hand. On the other hand, it was great Oscar was gone. It was a head trip: wanting to get back together versus my thoughts wondering if she even had enough time or energy to think about if she wanted to get back together. That mind game was always there, for a long time.

Tasha - 4

When I was in first grade, I used to think my life was perfect. I had great parents, a great house, awesome friends; nothing could go wrong. I was a normal kid having fun. Me, and my family living together under one roof was just perfect. It felt safe.

I remember that sometimes my parents would get mad at each other or me. They wouldn't leave me alone at the house but one would get in the car and leave and the other would go down to the patio. I would just watch TV by myself. When I'd get yelled at from my dad, my mom would always come and protect me and tell him he shouldn't yell, but just talk to me instead. Sometimes it would work, but sometimes it wouldn't work.

One day, I remember waking up and I just felt all gloomy like something could go wrong. Coincidentally, it was that day my parents told me; they were getting a divorce! Aghhh!

I felt like they were just doing this to make me mad. I was so angry at both of them. They told me they were still going to be friends, family, and everything. I felt better, but didn't know what to expect, because I didn't really understand what divorce was. I was sad for a little bit and confused.

Why are my parents divorcing?

I really didn't believe them because I thought divorce was really like couples not being nice to each other, never seeing each other, making the kid go between them. I was kind of scared about that, but then when it happened, my mom was just four blocks away from my dad's house and I could ride my bike over there if I wanted, just to go talk to which ever other person was there.

I remember moving into my second home. I hated it. "I want to go to my house." I would say, but my mom just said, "This is your home, too." That was when it hit me; *my parents are divorced*.

I remember feeling kind of weird about moving into someone else's bedroom. It was a boy's room; it was all white with splattered paint all over. But, I loved the idea of being able to decorate a whole new room. My dad's house is where I grew up and I was totally settled in. It's nice and spacious, and the same. But it was also kind of lonely. There is a big back yard with a pool, and a fire pit, and a swing set, it's my favorite. Both my beds are so comfy, but my closet was bigger at my mom's house. *(For a while, at least.)*

The one thing that helped me the most was a gift from my babysitter, my first grade journal. That journal let me write and draw out all my emotions. I just let out everything. To this day, I still have it. *(I don't write in it anymore).*

Going to school felt so awkward. I remember my teacher being there for me and telling me that if I ever needed someone to talk to she was always there. But I didn't want to tell any of my friends because I thought they'd think I'm weird and not like me anymore. Once I got comfortable, I told them and they were there for me. Just like my family, they were always calling and coming over to make me feel like nothing was wrong.

All my friends would ask me if my parents were mean to each other, what they fought about. And I'd say, "They haven't gotten into any fights. They are like best friends. They're like they're married, but don't live together and they don't wear wedding rings." It just felt nice, that they were friends.

At my dad's, I felt like *daddy's little princess*. At my mom's, I would have to do chores, like read and do my homework before I got to watch TV. But, my room was always a mess at my mom's. Sometimes I would clean it up.

My dad wasn't the perfect dad. He didn't know anything that he needed to know if I was going to live with him by myself. He needed to learn how to be a mom/dad and he did a pretty good job. Dad would make me read sometimes, but, he would just blow it off sometimes, too.

I get to do a lot of things at each of their houses that I don't get to do at the other one's house. I have fun… but, sometimes, I miss them together. I'm kind of happy they are divorced, but I'm also kind of sad. I'm happy that I have two different houses, and two different bedrooms. For school—I was on the same bus route, the same school and same friends… so that was good.

Then my mom met Oscar. Having Oscar in my life was definitely a good experience. I mean, Oscar was always there for me. I really liked him and he was really nice to me. He was from Venezuela. I went to the Park Spanish Immersion School and I would love to talk to him in Spanish without my mom knowing what we were talking about. He helped me with my Spanish homework. And, he made the best forts for me and my friends. It made me feel cool and funny.

Soon after, my dog died and that was hard because my mom wasn't there. She was out of town, I was at a birthday party, and my dad was the only one there with him, when Frankie died. My dad picked me up early, and I complained. I remember walking into the house, there was a blanket over him, and I saw my dog, dead. I remember calling my mom and her bawling on the phone... I missed him. He was my best friend since day one...

There was a stage when I wished my parents would get back together, when I'd always see moms and dads with their kids at PTA meetings and concerts. I mean, my parents always sat together, but it wasn't as if we were the 'typical family.'

I had those age periods where I just don't remember, but I don't forget that day I had two parents in my one house, because it was a big experience for me.

There was an air vent in my closet up to my mom's room and I could listen to her before I'd go to sleep. Sometimes I would just pretend that it was a new room at my dad's house and then I'd fall asleep.

I felt really bad when Oscar left. He didn't even say, "Goodbye..."

CHAPTER 4 DISCUSSION

Recognizing the 'Destructive Process'

It's fairly agreeable to most that no one wants to suffer, and for the most part, no one really wants to think of themselves as anyone who would inflict suffering upon another. Nevertheless, the fact is that being made of all the elements that make up the entire universe, we each have all the elements for the potential "good" and "evil."

There are a couple different analogies that I like to use to explain divorce, or any 'Relational Shift'—meaning something that changes from one definition to another.

I propose a major "Relational Shift" in one's life can be compared very much to the analogy of a major **surgery**.

When one is not "well," they may ignore or deny it until it becomes a devastating disease (consider the word in its parts, "Dis-Ease.") On the other hand, perhaps the "Dis-Ease" comes from a lack of nutrition or basic physical needs. An un-watered plant will soon wilt and die one leaf at a time.

Another potential may be the other extreme, where one thinks as a hypochondriac, and notices every little issue obsessively and compulsively, whether it really is an issue or not. This is still "Dis-Ease." At a certain point, there is no return to optimal health in any of these cases.

Think about it, why would we allow ourselves to continue "surviving" our lives when we can actually "live" them, with the pains and the pleasures of life?

In many traditions, they teach that suffering is based in fear. *If we fear and avoid change, or shifts in our relationships, than we actualize the stagnation of them.*

If we are to be consciously healthful of our states of "being," (meaning on the physical, mental, emotional and spiritual levels,) than we learn to attune to the "dis-harmonies" that are causing "Dis-Ease." When we consciously witness the natural evolution of all phenomena in the universe, (whatever its timeline,) then we will not overly suffer when a shift befalls our path. A child outgrows their shoes, a fetus outgrows the womb, a soul outgrows a life…

So, comparing these shifts to a surgery, with divorce as a primary example that is affecting millions of people and effecting great changes in our society, we can go into a surgery with as much information as possible, with as much help as we can muster for ourselves for the time during our recuperation, and setting up a rehabilitation plan.

Rather than mask the pains and ignore them until it is beyond repair, we can consciously understand that all in the universe is born, manifests its existence whether over millennia or in a flash of a millisecond, and then shifts into its next evolution. Energy is neither created nor destroyed; it only changes in form or frequency.

Either way, consciously planning for a surgery or having it hit you like a bus, when we recognize that our life is experiencing that surgery, how we go into it absolutely affects how we come out of it and our recovery.

Any "Dis-Ease" is infectious to some degree. When someone walks into a room and they are noticeably ready to fight, the energy in the room changes, everyone must be on guard. But all energy is resonant, and a person shining positive or harmonic energy entering a room will create an atmosphere that almost everyone will be attracted to and resonate with, gladly.

Extracting a relationship from our life, or shifting its placement so that its function is different than what it was before. "Relational Shifts" can be as scary and as painful as surgery, and require ample time for recovery, something many people avoid as long as possible. Then, when surgery is no longer avoidable, we act as though it came out of nowhere.

Divorce can affect a person's emotional, physical, mental, spiritual, financial, sexual, social, historical, and many other areas of one's total health.

The other analogy I use for any kind of "Relational Shift" the visualization of a birth. Any relationship may be exactly what we need in order for a seed to be planted within ourselves. That seed (idea, behavior, lifestyle...) gestates within the womb of the relationship. Eventually all wombs, or planters, are outgrown. When repotting a plant, dismembering it from the soil that has nourished it and held its roots sturdily in place, there is always the potential that the plant will not survive. Nevertheless, with tender care, that plant may not only endure, but has positive potential to actually thrive in its new planter, its new womb. But left its entire life in the same container, it can only grow so much.

Evocations:

1. Can we witness the "dis-harmonies" or "Dis-Eases" in our lives, or do we ignore our suffering, or growing pains, in an effort to avoid change?
2. When shifts seem to be unavoidable, do we prepare for them or wait until they've hit us like a bus, out of nowhere?
3. Can we be loving and grateful for the "womb" of a relationship, even when it is time to be expelled from it?
4. Can we take responsibility for our own health and not blame others for "infecting" us, when we directly put ourselves in the path of that "Dis-Ease?"
5. Are we seriously interested in taking the arduous task of living our lives **unabashedly alive**? Can we ever-evolve with the nature of nature?

CHAPTER FIVE

Rebuilding on the Ruins

Julie

Oscar came back to visit. It wasn't exactly stress free. There was a tiptoe-ing sort of tentativeness. At first, everything was in that haze that you go through when you are in love, and yet there was so much pressure. It was a very hard time.

Oscar was making this attempt to make a relationship with me work, which was what I had felt was so lacking in my previous marriage. He was willing to face the adversity and do what it took to make it work. We still had issues that we had to deal with, but he was making an effort to be there for me. There were still lies that needed to be cleared up, forgiven and let go of, but his visit was also lovely, and wonderful.

I went to visit him. I was prepared that it might end while I was there; if he felt we could only have a relationship if we were married. Instead, we had a dreamlike vacation week together with no pressures from him.

One evening, we went lobster hunting! It was the most exhilarating thing I had ever done in my life (although not nearly as scary as scuba diving at night!) Here I was across the world, with nothing but a pair of gloves, a snorkel and a stick. We had to come up for air, and then swim back down twenty feet under water, trying to find where the lobsters were. We'd come back up, re-create our strategy, and go back down. Working together to find our meal was as close to hunting as I'd ever been… not to mention, it was dangerous. I recognized that if I needed to hunt to feed my child or myself, I would probably be a very good huntress.

We caught two lobsters, but these were no ordinary lobsters from some fancy restaurant, these were each about 4 pounds! We put them on board the boat and dove back into the water. I kissed him underwater. Then I began to dance with him. We came up for air and went back down. He pulled me into him and spun me out just like on the dance floor.

When we finished, he said to me, "I've logged over 5000 hours under water in my life and I've never done anything like that. What you have exposed to me in this world is so beautiful. I'm so happy to have you in my life, however it might be."

We went on his friend's boat for a couple of nights. I loved driving the boat. It was so scary. It was the truest vacation from my life I think that I'd ever had. It was so romantic.

I left that trip having had such an amazing and rewarding time. I felt so alive with Oscar. As unsure as I was of him, I also felt safer than I ever had. *Why?*

We fell back in love, even though we were both terrified of it. Oscar continued to ask me to marry him. I felt good about a long distance relationship. He did not.

He threatened moving to the Republic of Micronesia. *Was he making that up? I found it. It's a real place. It's not even the size of a pinpoint on a map.* Another amazing life adventure to be had and I began to waiver. Nevertheless, I found my resolve. *He can go, but not marry me.*

I came back to my hectic life and prepared to go on the first family trip, post-divorce: Thanksgiving, 2001, in Palm Springs. Lee and I had not been living together for seven months, but our legal divorce was only a month fresh. Here we were taking a family trip together because, damnit, we're family and that was what we're going to continue to do. The family lifestyle, habits, and traditions that we had accumulated over all the years didn't really change just because we were divorced.

I still didn't feel a part of Lee and Tasha's loving, affectionate, incredible relationship; I still felt that I was there to simply support their life together. Even though I had divorced Lee, he was much more respectful to me on so many levels. Nevertheless, being with the two of them in a house, alone for a week without a group of friends (or any kind of outlet to get myself out of there when it was too painful,) only heightened my sensitivity to the fact that nothing had changed. Here I was again in our vacation home, feeling like an outsider in my own family, and it struck such deep chords in me that I went into the other room and called Oscar.

He made me feel better and soothed my aching heart. I told Oscar, "I'm ready to marry you. I'm ready to have a family with you. I'm ready to live a loving life with you." If I am able to admit my own shortcomings, I think I can look back now and admit this was partly out of desperation and very honestly, partly rebellious retaliation.

He was so excited, he was so happy, he was so thrilled. We sat on the phone and made plans for the most beautiful March wedding. It would be on a boat in the Cayman Islands. That was going to be his treat, his expense. We were going to invite friends down and whoever came, he was going to put them up. I could see the whole thing: I would be in a white bathing suit, with a gauze white veil flowing over me with all of our friends around. After the ceremony we would all jump into the water and play and splash and be merry; get married and be merry. *Oh, that was just such a beautiful fantasy.*

It all changed somehow. We ended up getting married a couple of weeks later. Oscar came to Minneapolis for his Christmas vacation. We discussed the practicalities of when he would move back in the coming spring after our wedding ceremony on the boat. The only problem would be that he wouldn't be able to work here for three months, meaning June.

This realized, we decided to get married while he was in town so all the immigration paperwork would be done by the time he returned. I hadn't told very many about my March wedding plans yet, they were still so fresh, but I never thought of hiding it. But… now the wedding would be in two weeks? *Oy gavult…*

I was resolved, if I was going to get married, then it wouldn't be under secrecy. I was no longer going to live my life with secrets. *What was I thinking??*

So, on the coldest day of the year, twenty degrees below zero, we had this beautiful wedding. Tasha was my flower girl. When I look at the pictures of that day, I see she was truly excited and happy. When asked who was giving me away, I proudly said, "I'm giving myself away, this time." *Do we hear what we say?*

We stayed up the night before cooking. God, he was a good cook. We made cream puff balls, we made incredible pasta, and we made such delectable delights. We were laughing all night. It was just so much fun. We cleaned the whole kitchen, made it all ready for our big wedding the next day.

My dear niece had flown in to be here for the wedding. She stayed up cooking with us until she couldn't go any longer. We were manic with excitement and were not tired at all. She slept in Tasha's room, which has a vent that directly connects to my upstairs bathroom.

Oscar, in his mischievous humor-eerily like Lee's—knowing my niece was afraid of ghosts, laid down next to my vent and crooned spookily into the vent, calling her name. We could hear her calling my name quietly, "Julie…?" Then, screaming, she ran upstairs to find us both in tears, laughing on the ground next to the vent. She couldn't help but laugh because it was contagious, our exuberance and lightness. I felt a little guilty, but to be honest, I still laugh just writing about it.

Oscar and I did have a little spat that next morning of the wedding. He wasn't happy with the shoes that he had to wear with the suit that I had bought for him. I, of course, had paid for everything for the wedding.

He was still going to pay for the one in Cayman, and for all our friends to come down and stay there. Whoever could make it, he would treat like royalty. That was a really generous plan!

The night before, while we were cooking, it had snowed. That morning, it was pure ice out on the roads, but Oscar had to go buy a new pair of shoes. I said, "It just doesn't matter, you could have an accident and then what?"

"I want to get a new pair of shoes now! You're not going to stop me." He was being very defiant and we (my friends that had come to help set up or take pictures or do my hair,) all just backed off. Was he getting truly cold feet?

Again, another little red flag, but what to do? We're going to work through these things. We're going to have the perfect life. We'll have some disagreements but we can get past them. Everyone would be here in an hour, but he insisted on leaving, so I said, "Okay I hope you make it back in time for the ceremony."

Of course, he did return in time, and he had gotten beautiful shoes.

Those people that loved me and wanted to be a part of my life, other than Lee of course, all came to celebrate my wedding to this man that we all thought was going to be the man of my dreams. How romantic that we had found each other and what a struggle we had gone through, but we were going to make it work. It was truly one of those days where everyone was encompassed in this high-love.

I think I looked the most beautiful that I had looked in ages on that day. I had bought myself this fantasy, gorgeous, fairy-looking dress that was three sizes too big for me but I didn't care. I pinned it up, I tucked it in; I made it work. With sheer joy, I walked down the aisle and gave myself away.

During the ceremony, poor Oscar choked. He couldn't say the words, "Till death do us part." The third try, he finally got half the sentence out and the judge was like, "Okay, that's good enough."

At first, he really did continue to cater to me. We had a lovely, lovely wedding night at a hotel that he got through one of his friends. However, the next morning as we were leaving he said to me, "I have a surprise for you for our wedding... I'm not going back to Cayman."

I realized he had once again shown up with all his possessions, less a few scuba things. He explained that one off so reasonably. He knew he was returning in a few months, and there was no reason to bring everything back and forth. And, what if one of his roommates might steal some of his stuff? He just didn't want to leave it there when he knew he was coming back. Now that he didn't have to go back, it was a good omen that he had all his stuff with him.

Now, the plan was that he was going back. We were going to visit each other once a month for a week. Then, during spring break, we would have another ceremony, the fantasy one that we had talked about. This ceremony had been spontaneous.

He told me, now that he was married, it was more important to start his new life. He reassured me that there were plenty of people to cover him at work. I was surprised, because I knew that it was the busiest time of year for their business. I said, "You're not going to be able to find a job in Minnesota, right now."

"Trust me, I can do it. Trust me," he said. After all, it was his home and I was his wife. He was going to stay, and he was going to get his permit, his green card, and find a job.

He soon realized that the week before Christmas was not the week to try to find a job, much less find anybody in the office to even discuss a job.

I was trying to make this new marriage work inside my old life, but they clashed like speeding cars on a raceway on so many levels. My marriage to Oscar happened so quickly that I can only say I blinked, and there we were. He was back in my home, spending my money, not working, and demanding sex half a dozen times a day; then pouting when he didn't get it. I was on a pendulum swing from hardly any sex to hardly any time outside of it to get on with my life.

I had to ask myself, *just what was I willing to do for this thing called, "In love"?* How much would I risk to 'have it all'? My family suffered through my inquiry.

A few in my (very large,) immediate family were having a hard time with everything. There was a holiday dinner that I was welcome to come to alone, or with Lee and Tasha. Oscar was not welcome. Period. I didn't know what to do about it.

It was so difficult to manage everyone's feelings. I had chosen to spend my life with Oscar, yet, I didn't want to lose the loving relationships I had with my nieces and nephews. I went alone, but only stayed long enough to kiss each of the children and give them their gifts. Lee felt I shouldn't have even gone at all. He felt I had married someone, and my family should invite my husband, whether they liked him or not. I suffered from it, but knew they were basing their actions from what they thought was right. It still was extremely painful.

It was a very tough time on me ..., on Oscar..., on Lee... and, of course, on Tasha. That kind of stress just escalated the situation. Oscar would go back and forth between being so supportive, loving, and giving, to being so obstructive, hurtful, and needy. He would still do sweet things, like drawing a bath and giving me a rub down, or leave me tender cards with the most thoughtful sentiments. He kept trying to fatten me up and would cook for me. *I must have that male thing in me, a way to get to my heart, or in my pants, is to feed me well.*

Like ripples move through water, little gestures can have major effects on all that is touched by them. Somehow, through our philosophical discussions (between Lee and me, as well as between Oscar and me,) Lee came around to inviting Oscar and I to dinner. He felt it was up to him to emulate what we had promised Tasha, that we were still family, no matter what. Buddha? I think he also relished in my squeamishness at sitting with Oscar on the couch. He said, *"Don't mind me, you can sit together and hold hands. Really, I mean it. Don't mind me…"* Yes, it was still good to know I could always trust his words.

I was trying to find balance now that Oscar was back in my life. I have constantly challenged myself to stretch my limitations emotionally and spiritually, and I have had to deal with several bruises in my vigorous workouts. My second marriage was doomed from the start, but we had high hopes.

Oscar and I were on a manic ride to "happily ever after' but we were foreseeably going to crash to all but ourselves. We thought we were going to sail through life's problems together undeterred, a force to be reckoned with if you got in our way… *Am I having deja vu here, or what?*

It is very easy for people to experience seasonal affective disorder here in Minnesota when the days are bitter cold, short, and dark and there is no sun.

I recognized that Oscar was going through a depression and I was getting very concerned. Oscar was a man who had lived his whole life on an ocean, or, at least near a beach and close to the equator. Sure, shoveling snow for the first time was fun, but by the tenth time, it's a fricking chore. It's darn cold out and it sucks.

He was experiencing the winter blues. He wasn't getting the work that he wanted to get. His confidence was going down each day and my asking him questions didn't help; another similarity to my first marriage. "What happened to all the money you said you were bringing up here? I'm supporting you and you're not being a partner with me. You're kind of living off me… Just what is the truth here? What is happening?"

He was very skillful, but I was becoming less and less blinded by love, shall we say? I became more realistic each month, as I had to do my bills and he was contributing a few hundred dollars as opposed to half of whatever our monthly costs were.

Every day there was another argument that had to be contended. Much of it had to do with our sex life. *How I had set myself up for that!*

I thought it was all in his head that we didn't have enough sex because statistically, we did. I had to experience what I put Lee through--even though I was having the condensed version, in a matter of weeks, rather than years and years.

His personality was beginning to change in front of my eyes and it got to the point, where, I was dreading coming home to my own house because I didn't know what to expect.

Lee asked me, "What's the difference, you just married another man and you're still living the same life. What about all the dreams you said you had? What about all the other reasons you said you didn't want to be married, like being stifled in a marriage, and yet, here you are, married. I don't see any difference, except that you have more sex."

This was haunting, because there were a lot of differences, some of which I really didn't want to admit, like that this man was living off of me and thinking I'm some rich divorcee. Maybe in his eyes I was, but in my community, I was far from being a rich divorcee.

I still didn't want to say that my marriage to him was a mistake, but I was recognizing that it was going to be a challenge to be with him. When we went to this homeopathic doctor, he recognized right away that Oscar was very, very ill. I don't think that he was able to give Oscar the right medicine.

Lee and I talked. He was the one that I needed to express my fears to. However, I couldn't really tell him all of the things that were going on because, you know, we didn't talk about sex. We never have, so I couldn't really talk to him about a problem that I was having with another man, at this stage.

As for the money, I knew that he was worried about me financially. He knew that the stock market was falling. In addition, he knew I'd lost most of what I was left with, and yet I didn't want him to feel responsible for taking care of me. I had moved on, and it was not his responsibility to take care of me. Therefore, I couldn't really talk about the whole money issue either.

We still had big differences about how to raise Tasha, so that was a tentative subject as well.

I suppose the easiest subject that we could discuss was our families. That's where he and I were family. It was special that we could be that person for one another; the one who knew almost the whole background of the last couple of decades.

Lee and I continued to talk daily, much to the chagrin of others, especially Oscar. Lee and I would struggle through those hard conversations but recognized that we were living through them, consciously awake. Yep, some of them put us in a tizzy, but we had really made a much better commitment to each other in our divorce than we did in our marriage.

The end of my marriage to Oscar's was like one of those bombs that you see coming right at you. You hear the whistle and yet you don't move, you don't run for cover, you just recognize that this is what is coming.

That was what was happening. I knew I was going to live and deal with the circumstances …or it would kill me.

I don't think that I had the clarity to see as big of a picture as, obviously, hindsight allows me to see now. I know that my wanting to marry him was once again a desperate attempt at feeling loved, and the only place that I was really feeling it was from him, even if it was painful. I felt loved by friends and much of my family, but I was in need of that all-encompassing fantasy of a partner-for-life kind of loving; someone who would stand next to me, side-by-side.

It only took a few months before Oscar's symptoms of depression surfaced and the destroyer in him overpowered.

After having worked all day, I returned home to a messy house and an unkempt, drunk husband who became defiant and defensive with every concern I had. "Honey, I'm worried about you," I said while picking up clothes and dishes, as he watched.

"This is not working out…why aren't you at work? I'm drained." I told him. He sat up and disdainfully and defiantly glared at me with eyes of steel. His eyes were the most expressive of anyone I'd ever known. Moreover, they would change color with his moods. Crystal blue clear sparkling when he felt love, greener than a moor when he was lying and steel grey when he was ready to pounce. His words struck, "Everyday I'm waiting for you to say you want a divorce."

I was stunned. I had done so much to prove my love. Everyday he would add something to the list, "If I really loved him …" I was expected to "prove" that I loved him. Well, that's a lose-lose situation. "So, everyday you are testing me to see how far you can push it?"

His nearly schizophrenic, bipolar, manic-depressive state became more than he or I could contain. I raised the white flag and asked for a divorce after only four months of marriage. I realized he would never be what he had presented and promised to me. I wanted to crawl under a rock and hide from the world. I realized, *I'm going to be twice divorced within one year.* What were the chances? Who could be that dumb? ME!

Oscar left to go to a friend's house. I spent the night pulling his things together and folding them, smelled his smell of ocean and lust. It had been the only place in years where I felt I could sleep wrapped in someone's arms. I allowed myself some time to grieve.

I spent the rest of the dark morning hours packing his things, suppressing my anger and thoughts of throwing his things out on the lawn. I was almost through when the last drawer revealed something so horrible that the fury inside me blew out. I didn't want to believe what I found was what I feared. I could barely get myself to take it out of the drawer much less put it in the VCR.

He had promised me there were no copies. He promised that he had sent me the original and I would never have to worry about it again in my life. The biggest lie of them all, I only needed one second to recognize it was a copy.

I screamed a scream that only a Yiddish word can express… I 'shrayed.'

Shraying starts like a vowel sung at the lowest note you can possibly exert and raises in pitch and volume until it sounds like a screeching banshee. There is no controlling it once it has begun. Something cracks and the chaos of the universe boils up and out from within you.

I found myself pulling the yards and yards and yards of tape out of the cassette. It wouldn't stop coming, like all the fears of… how many others were made? Who has them? Was he going to use this to blackmail me?

Insanity came over me forsaking my breath, the calmness and the love. I wanted to thrash him to bits. I realized the only probable truth he ever told me was how everyone that had loved him eventually threw him out. I was no longer above that, no longer able to ride the wave of love into a deeper sense of compassion for all his losses. He had obviously earned each one.

It wasn't my problem. He finally did have a job and his own money. I did not need to worry about anything, except that he might still be able to get money, not only from me but… from Lee! My name was still on the title of his house!! "Oh God, don't let him be able to get money from Lee, too."

That was it. I would never allow myself to be "in love" again! It was a drug, and I was going to beat it. I could love, but to be "in love" was to be drugged with a paper bag over the head, not seeing the obvious flaws of this cubic zirconium, saccharin-sweet thing. It was no diamond and it did not last the test of time. It faked itself into being what it thought was real and yet could not stand the heat that melted its flawfulness. In full view of those who were sold by its brilliance, the clarity melted into a boiling mass of sticky toxic ooze.

Oh! How was I going to get through this one? I had already worn the scarlet letter all over town this last year, and thought I had gotten through it, past it. But who knew what was coming next? This tape could ruin even more of my life. Not that the whole community hadn't already known the superficial story, that I had left my husband of seventeen years for my Latin aficionado and married him within months of my divorce. I had put my child through the whole thing--with everyone she met looking at her with pity that whole year. How would I explain this to her, *at not even nine years old?*

In my humiliation, I leave the house and head for downtown. I expect my lawyer friend to condescend to me, "Julie how could you not see this coming?" Or, "How could you not have a prenuptial agreement?" I knew this would come up. All the questions that all the voices in my head were beating me up with, I was sure this lawyer would ask.

Actually, he was as kind as an old comforter. He had no appearance of judgment or disdain. He actually seemed to feel for me. He told me I needn't worry about divorcing him and reassured me that Oscar would not be able to get his hands on Lee's home or money. My relief allowed my stomach to unravel just a bit, but my feet were cramping from my inability to release my clenched toes. My short breath exacerbated the lightheadedness, but I was compelled to continue to figure out what I needed to do to unravel the rest of this mess.

I next went to the free county attorney's desk and waited in line for an hour with crying babies, irritated mothers and scary looking fathers. I realized I had to breathe or I would collapse from a lack of sleep and an overdose of adrenaline in the last twelve hours.

Oh my God, the clerk at the courthouse recognized me. She turned to me and said, "Don't worry honey; you've already done it once, so this time should be easy." She winked. I crept out of there, paperwork in hand, and went home. I parked in the driveway knowing I would have to walk in the front door. I had locked the house up for the first time ever—I didn't want him coming in while I was gone. I worked on the divorce papers the rest of the day. The puppy, Junior, was driving me crazy, barking non-stop the whole afternoon. I needed to give him attention. I tried to throw his ball, but just couldn't take the piercing bark and he wouldn't stop. I finally left him outside, barking and scratching at the door. I was going insane from it. I had to get this paperwork done and turned in to the courthouse the next day.

When I finally finished, the clock showed 7 p.m. I called Oscar, but he didn't answer. I left a message, "Okay, I've got the paperwork done… I want this over with as soon as possible, so call me and tell me where to come and get your signature." He never called back.

At that point, I felt like a drink. I rarely drink. A friend of mine was singing with her band in a local club. I freshened up, but not as if I was trying to look good for anyone… that was not going to be the case anymore. I was not going to powder, paint, and make myself what I ain't just to have a guy look at me and think I might be the girl of his dreams. Take me as I am. I will not change myself anymore just to be loved by another. *Funny, isn't that what Lee asked of me a hundred times?*

Now that I was sure he wouldn't be able to get any more money from me, or any from Lee, I felt I deserved some time to let loose all the tension that had built up. I backed out of my driveway and drove about 40 feet before realizing that I had forgotten to lock the garage side door. I was clearly suspicious, maybe more afraid, that Oscar might resort to something crazy. I didn't want to come home after drinking and find him in my garage waiting for me. I had to lock it.

I reached for the handle and it burned my hand. Panic quickly swept over me as I called out to Oscar and slowly opened the door. A rush of burning air blasted me.

I ran away thinking, *he's going to kill me, it's going to explode!*

Oscar was a trained mercenary on top of everything else. He was able to kill in the most efficient or gruesome way. He was also taught the ways to die and had told me more than once that he would die by drowning. The asphyxiation allowed one to feel euphoric before they died, and since he loved the ocean so dearly, he always waited for the day when he would let himself run out of air by some beautiful coral reef...

My garage did not compare to this vision, with its tools and garbage cluttering the space. He had placed a board over the broken windowpane. Nailed it in tight. Slats were covering the spaces under the doors. A 2 x 4 short plank was lodged into the gas pedal of his car.

He committed suicide in my garage.

Lee rushed over, thinking my frightened call was in fear of Oscar hurting me. The next heroic thing I witnessed Lee do was that moment where he was in that painful place once again, of trying to revive someone, not knowing if they were already dead. However, this time it wasn't our beloved dog that would claim the nature of his true character, it was my second husband whom Lee dragged from the car and laid gently to the ground. He shook him, "Wake up, don't do this to her!" Then, he started to listen for a heartbeat. He looked up at me and yelled, "Call 911."

It suddenly struck me that I had called him first without even calling the police. The atmosphere started to swirl around me as I heard myself telling Lee not to try to revive him. "Let him die, that's what he wanted all along."

My body crumbled to the ground. We didn't know how long he'd been there. I couldn't imagine being tied to a vegetable for however long he would live, if he survived and had brain damage. He wouldn't want that.

Last time when I had told him to leave, Oscar begged me for another chance. When I didn't give it to him, he claimed it gave him the anger needed to take his life back and to enjoy it with me or without me. That was the person I fell 'in love' with, the one who saw the beauty and potentiality in life. This time, he knew there was no possibility of my ever trusting him again. He knew he could not trust himself. He did love me, and knew I loved him… The healthy part of him knew, I think.

This time, my not taking him back gave him what he needed to finally take his life. Holy shit.

The paramedics arrived with their sirens screeching and took over the CPR from Lee. I ached as the wails of lost eternity emerged from my depths. Lee came to me, shaking visibly. He was crying…for me. A few times, when Oscar was not reviving, he shook his shoulders and yelled at him, "Don't do this to her, you fucker!" Lee was reeling with guilt that he had somehow put all this upon me, that it was his entire fault.

At some later point, the police told me they were taking his body away and asked if I wanted to say goodbye. I could not feel my mind inside my body, but my body was still working on my behalf. My feet carried me out to the driveway. My legs allowed me to kneel down beside his now cold body. I hadn't seen him close up yet.

Since Oscar's mother had abandoned him at 4-years-old, he had been waiting for this day almost all his life and the smile on his face at meeting his Creator was indescribable. There was such joy, such awe, such gratitude and there was relief in his eyes that sparkled crystal blue. There was a smile that was discreetly, but undeniably, there. It was the face of a man dying from a cosmic orgasm!

I thanked him for leaving my life, for not continuing to haunt me for years to come, but mostly I thanked him for not taking me with him, nor my child, or her father. I realize he could have easily taken any of us with him if he had wanted to harm me even more.

This was his final and only way to tell me he loved me.

He told me how dying underwater makes you feel high from the loss of oxygen, giddy even. His look was not giddy.

I can still see it clearly, years later. Rather than it haunting me, it comforts me. It made me think he was greeted by a host of angels, who bringing him to God, told him that he did a good job; he paid his dues and got to come Home, to love, and to rest his mind and soul.

I walked through the sliding door and felt so many people in the window watching me. I realized I had lost about an hour with all of the commotion. Suddenly it seemed there were a couple dozen of my closest friends there. I didn't know how they got there or found out about Oscar so fast.

It was an eerie sensation of deja vu from twenty years earlier when I was in "West Side Story." At that point, I finally had a chance to cry out loud over my own father's death and the fact that I was being watched allowed me to share my pain with the spectators whom all knew of my recent loss. There had not been a dry eye in the theatre, nor was there now, behind the sliding door.

There, sitting in the corner of my dining room was the lawyer I had seen only hours ago. How did he get here? Who called him?

He saw me notice him, waved off my gratitude and explained that he spoke Spanish and could help with calling Oscar's family in Venezuela. I didn't know what to say to his family. I wanted to thrash them all for creating such a sad and lonesome soul, but it wasn't their fault. I wanted to get my hands on his mother. She should know her abandonment eventually killed her son's will to live. She was to blame, not me. Not me. Not me.

The police were curious why I called Lee--before them.

Lee - 5

Rebuilding. Wow, an ongoing process. Oscar was a category seven hurricane, but not the earthquake. Our relational shift had in some way made us stronger together and apart. No, we did not implode.

When Julie told me she was going to remarry, my initial thought was that she left me for another man, which hurt my ego, terribly. I specifically remember telling family members and friends that she was nuts. I didn't have to explain that to anyone.

What the hell is she doing now?

She wanted to get married right away. Too bad, so sad. I did feel bad for her, though. I thought that she was marrying him more for the necessity of it than the want. Yes, she did love him, but to marry him? No, she needed time to be alone.

However, Julie does as Julie wants to do--that is one of her greatest traits, one I most admire, and one that I am afraid of most. I always had the fear of change. *I still have the fear of change.*

Julie is a person that needs and wants to be loved. She is a loved person.

But something hit her down in Palm Springs after we had separated. When she saw how Tasha and I were still having fun, she felt left out and that made her mad. She lost it and suddenly, out of nowhere, wanted to marry Oscar. There was nothing that I did to intentionally hurt her. If being myself and being a father, being happy, laughing, giggling and playing with my daughter was going to make her get married to Oscar, well then, you know, it's her life. She could do with it whatever she wanted.

A couple in her family were against supporting her, but many more supported her lovingly. Some of her friends were telling her not to marry him and some were excited for her. The one thing I give her credit for is that she told me she would not wait so long to leave Oscar if things were not what she thought they should be. I loved her honesty with me. It hurt, yes. Honesty, always.

Oscar fell in love with a woman, happened to be my wife, but he fell in love with a wonderful, spiritual woman. He was obviously unstable, but Julie couldn't see anything like that at the time.

Tasha was the purpose of why I had to remain strong and positive. She was a young girl, and she had a lot of opinions surfacing. People thought the way I was giving her attention was wrong, that I was too focused on her. But, you know, my prime objective was to make sure that she came out of this okay, and me, too.

As hard as it was, there was no alternative, none. I wanted to teach my daughter how not to be mean, cold, and angry, causing more pain. It was a much more important lesson to be civilized.

As time went by, I saw that Oscar wasn't just a "thing," and that he was going to be in Tasha's life. It just got to the point that I needed to get to know this person a little better. After all, he was living with my daughter. I remember seeing him once through Julie's window, not very clearly. I made a decision that I was going to invite the both of them over to my house for dinner.

I don't remember the dinner much. One of the things I do recall is walking downstairs with Oscar to the bar to get a couple of shots of scotch to calm us down a little. We just hung out that night, ate a great meal, played games. It was nice when the two of them left. It definitely sucked.

I lost Julie as a wife, but I wanted to keep her in my life as a friend.

Julie never really shared her personal side with Oscar with me. All I heard was what a great cook he was and how handy he was, and that he was redoing the home they were going to be living in. Oscar moved into a strange country, strange surroundings, and the last thing he needed was an ex-husband that got along with his ex-wife.

I saw him as a normal person doing what he was doing. He was always nice to Tasha. Tasha never told me anything bad about him. They were a married couple starting a life under situations of the most duress. I distanced myself on purpose to give them a chance to have a life.

I pointed the fingers towards me and Julie pointed the fingers towards her. So we both took a lot of responsibility and blame. We each had sympathy for the other. Neither of us wanted to hurt or harm the other, but it happened...

I didn't even know that they were having marital issues. I didn't have information because it was Julie and Oscar's life. When Julie first called me up and told me about Oscar, that she planned to divorce him, again I felt I was partly to blame for what she was going through. They were like two buses pushing against one another, not going anywhere...

As bad as I felt for her though, inside I was happy.

There was a piece of me that was somewhat relieved, just crazy thoughts inside of my head, fantasy thoughts in my head you know? The door was open, and the game might be on again. I thought heck, maybe I can swoop in and get my family back together. Now that he was not going to be around anymore, I felt that it would be extremely beneficial for her to take some time, find out more about herself.

Not to forget, of course, there was that moment of complete frustration when it's just, "Aahg!" Tasha would have to go through a divorce again. Obviously, it turned out a lot worse than anybody could have imagined.

I remember getting a phone call sometime during the evening. Tasha and I had been out and were just settling down. Tasha answered the phone and kept asking if everything is Okay. "Who is on the phone?" I asked.

"It's Mom, she needs to talk to you real bad." I got on the phone and Julie was pretty much in hysterics. She wanted me to come there right away. She mentioned Oscar by name, but I could not understand what she said. I asked her if I should bring Tasha, and she whispered, "No."

I knew something bad was going on. I wasn't exactly sure what, but something terrible had happened.

So I asked our neighbors if they could watch her, and sped away in my car. We are usually about 5 minutes away--I probably made it there in about a minute, but during that minute, my adrenaline started pumping so hard. I was ready for whatever he was doing to Julie. I was ready to just go and beat the pulp out of him. I thought he had hit her. I thought she was locked inside the house.

I remember vividly driving up her street and about a block away, I could see her sitting on her lawn. When I pulled into her driveway, she ran up to me. She was crying, "He's in there, he's in there."

I'm yelling, "Where is he? Where is he? What has he done to you?"

She kept pointing to the garage and I noticed that the car that Julie had bought him was there. I saw for the first time the shadow of the back of his head in the driver's seat. I went over to him, not knowing anything yet. When I saw him, it hit me that he was trying to kill himself, committing suicide. He committed suicide.

When I walked into the garage, it definitely had a stench of exhaust fumes. I went to the side of the truck and saw he was slumped with his head leaning back against the window. I opened the front passenger door and I saw there was a two by four jimmied between the chair and the accelerator. At that point, I turned around and yelled to Julie, "Dial 911! Now!"

I took the keys from the ignition and pulled Oscar out thinking he was maybe still alive. I dragged him to the driveway to get him some fresh air. I tried to revive him by mouth-to-mouth resuscitation. I remember, vividly, yelling and swearing at him to "Wake the fuck up! Do not do this to Julie and Tasha!"

I kept hearing this noise come out of his mouth. I couldn't feel a pulse, but his eyes were open and he had this kind of smile on his face. I wasn't sure if he was dead, or not.

I found out later on that when you give a person who is already dead mouth-to-mouth resuscitation, the air that comes out passes through the vocal cords and makes a moaning sound, which was what I heard.

I looked up at Julie who was sitting outside, crying hysterically. I couldn't even imagine what she must have been thinking watching her ex-husband try to revive her current husband who she is just about to divorce. It was just an unreal atmosphere. Then, you could hear the sirens approaching.

There were at least a couple of squad cars, an ambulance and a big old fire truck. They pulled me out of the way and did their thing. They gave him those electric shocks and after five to ten minutes, they gave up. By that time, a crowd had gathered at the end of the driveway.

The police did question Julie and me. In fact, we got a bit of a suspicious look from an officer. With me being the ex-husband, they wondered why she called me before them. They asked me not to leave town until the investigation was over. It was somewhat funny, but not really. When you know you are an innocent person, you don't have anything to worry about and I knew I didn't do anything, so I kind of laughed it off.

Friends and family started coming over. Everybody there was worried and wanted to make sure that Julie was okay. Nobody really gave a shit about me or at least that's the way I felt, and that's okay. It really wasn't about me, but it was one of the first times where I really felt I was an ex-husband.

Once the police were done with me and I knew that Julie was surrounded by her friends, I knew that I could go home and get Tasha. She was almost asleep, but I picked her up. As I was carrying her back to my house, the only thing she kept asking me was, "Is Mommy okay? Is Mommy okay?" I mean, my God, was I ever crying on the inside after all the things this girl has been going through.

I assured her that Mommy was well, and that she would be here in the morning. I could not, could not, and did not want to be the one to tell her about Oscar. I really wanted Julie to be here to assure Tasha that her mom and dad are here for her no matter what.

The following morning was tough. We had to explain to Tasha, then an eight-year-old, what suicide is, and why people do it...And why we thought Oscar did. You can't just say, *he died.* We had to be honest with her and explain it to her. *You have to.* We did, and I believe we did discuss everything we needed to, at that time.

There was pain for Julie too. I hoped she wasn't feeling responsible for him. I feared the "I told you so's" that she was going to go through with some of her family would be difficult. It was tough, just going through the pain again for all of us. It had barely been over a year since she left.

Most of everything I learned about Oscar came after his suicide. I did know that he got a job working as a diver in Bayport or Stillwater, somewhere. I knew there were some money issues, but not to the point of thinking this guy was nuts, or going to commit suicide, or that my daughter and Julie might be in some sort of danger...no clue.

I had no knowledge of the lies, the money, that he drank a lot, that he was bipolar, or that he couldn't get enough sex (which is pretty ironic.) I had no knowledge about the tape or her pregnancy. I didn't know any of that stuff until after he died. It did worry me, after finding all this out, that Tasha had been in the same house as him, and that Julie had dealt with this day in and day out right after we split. *She's a glutton for punishment, I'll agree.*

The week before he committed suicide, I found it strange that he was walking Tasha's new dog, Junior, in front of my house. I yelled out to him, "Oscar! Hey!"

I don't remember the conversation, only that it struck me odd to see him. Maybe, in Oscar's jealousy of my relationship with Julie, he was checking up to see if she was over, or not.

Tasha - 5

I had wanted a sibling. I mean, when I would go on vacations, I didn't like being an only child because you get bored very easily. I would see pictures of my friends with their brothers and their sisters. They, like, hang out with each other while they are on vacations. Those moments made me want a sibling.

When my mom told me she was getting married to Oscar, the first thing I can remember saying to her was, "Can I be the flower girl"? I was pretty happy that I got to be a flower girl. It seriously had been a dream of mine to be a flower girl.

I was never going to call him my step dad, because I really didn't consider him a step dad, but he was a really good friend and everything.

I didn't really notice it, but my mom told me he was acting really strange and lying a lot. Sometimes, she told me what he lied about. I was like, "Why would Oscar do that?" Then I figured out why. He was really depressed.

Then one night, I was at my dad's house. The phone rang and I answered it. My mom was screaming. I thought someone had a knife or a gun in her house, but she said it wasn't. So my dad sent me to my neighbor's house and my dad told her dad, but he wasn't allowed to tell me what was going on. I just hung out with my friend and acted like nothing was wrong. My dad had told me my mom was just locked out.

That night he told me, "Yeah, she got locked out; she was just scared because the dog was barking." My reaction was, "Oh, okay." However, in the morning, they didn't send me to school. They told me.

Oscar committed suicide.

I didn't cry. I felt kind of bad, but I also didn't … See, I was mad that he didn't say good-bye to me or my mom, and that he would do that at my mom's house. He didn't say good-bye the first time he left, either, but this time was forever.

I think Oscar's suicide was one of my first encounters with the death of someone I was close to. Oscar was living with me and it's kind of weird to have someone living with you one day, and then gone the next second. Kind of like the divorce, except my parents never left me. That's a big difference.

I don't think that I understood as much as I could probably understand now about what went on, but I know that I was open to whatever my parents told me.

CHAPTER 5 DISCUSSION

*Recognizing What's Useful and
What Needs to Go*

One person must actually make *the move* and is usually seen as 'the bad guy.' However, many avoid surgery--waiting, instead, for death to release them from the self-designed prison they have created for themselves, rather than walk out of an unlocked door. This way, the finger can be pointed outward, saying that the other did this or that to ruin everything.

If we look at the pointing hand, we will see three fingers pointing right back at ourselves. This is a traditional form of self-discovery therapy. When we point a finger outward, are we willing to accept there are at least three things of ourselves that we could witness of the same behavior or that brought us down this path to encounter this issue presenting itself? Either way, we all set up our little destructions so that we can move on, I believe.

When mental, spiritual, or emotional illness pervades a loved one, we are called to be aware and offer help, even though the disappointments attached to that illness may surface. Nonetheless, we need to cultivate practices of resilience, fortitude and courage to ward off the invasive illness that could resonate its "Dis-harmonies" into our own "vibes," just as we follow precautions with physical "Dis-Eases," by washing our hands frequently or various other practices.

Again, looking at relationships as *wombs* for our gestation into our next evolution, we can be aware of the shifts. Perhaps with age and experience, we can recognize when the weather will turn by the broken bone flaring discomfort years after the injury has healed. If an injury never healed properly, than perhaps scar tissue binds all that surrounds it. We can think of our mental, emotional and spiritual scars of past wounds that seem to arise under the "right conditions."

Perhaps relationship after relationship repeat our patterns and we have only to witness them and practice, practice, practice the natural process of selection, deciding which plants to cultivate, and which to weed, repot or move into better light… This process of self-improvement, rebirth and renewal is met by accepting the challenges in our lives as the opportunity to practice.

You can not get into the ring without months of training, after all.

Each shift allows us to practice "right action" while releasing whatever isn't working anymore. The entire world is experiencing shifts on all levels. There is an emergent awareness looking to the future, and preparing for it by cleansing and purifying old injuries, thoughts, and behaviors that have kept our minds bound to powerlessness. Millions are working to find their power and purpose and to express it with integrity and compassion, recognizing there will be painful moments during the laborious trials of being reborn while you are alive in this form.

Learning to use our minds in conjunction with our feelings requires us to visualize potential situations and then to "feel, or sense" how the body reacts.

Noticing where we "feel" our fears, our compassion, exhilaration, depths and everything in between is a phenomenon that we as humans are capable of experiencing. The ability to feel our emotions in our body and our breath, allows us to practice, and thereby apply, when in a situation where we may catch ourselves reacting from fears. We can then analyze if that is the appropriate feeling being attached to the situation, or question if it is from past injury that may not have healthfully healed.

<u>Evocations:</u>

1. How do I define "true love?" Does that equate to "unconditional love?" What are the "conditions" of true love?
2. What do I feel I can or must count on in life? What would I do if that changed?
3. Do I feel guilt from inflicting feelings of abandonment on others? Am I imprisoned by my own attachments to having been abandoned?
4. Is there anyone out there who has not experienced being both the "bad guy" and the "good guy?"
5. What practices do I perform to "cleanse" my spirit and emotions and thoughts, as I would shower the dirt of the day off my body?
6. When my patterns arise in front of me once again, do I continually blame others for it still presenting itself to me?
7. Am I able to attune to my own "feelings" and name them?
8. Am I able to catch myself when reacting from previous injury rather than the incident at hand?

CHAPTER SIX

Letting the Dust Settle

Julie

Funny thing widow-ship, one moment you're just a normal crazy person, and then boom, people's eyes change size and moisten when they see you. All of the sudden, I was someone to pity. Until they would hear that I had kicked him out of the house that day, then they were not so sure I was so pitiful. What could I have said *to get a man to kill himself?*

Hey, one too many lies..., big lies...His fabrications posed unknown dangers and revealed others around every corner. It was amazing how many started to pop up daily after his death. It was unbelievable that he was able to keep them all going for so long, that he was able to keep them all straight for so long. Just who was he, really?

It had been several weeks since I had become widowed.

Everyday during this digestive period, I would take a pile of his things, start to clean them out and find, say, a pay stub from one of his checks from when he was working in Cayman. It showed that he was actually making about one fourth of what he told me he had been earning. That was not the issue; I didn't care what he was earning.

It was that a.) He lied to me about it--for nothing but some fear, and b.) He used the lie to shame me that he had left this great paying job to come here.

When I did finally go to Cayman, to see if there really were any of these supposed properties he spoke about, or if his bank accounts or possessions he'd left behind even existed. I was able to meet up with his boss and a co-worker. They were very kind to me. I was afraid they would think I lured him into his wretched destiny, like a siren instead of the treasure he had claimed I was. It turned out he had left them high and dry (on the ocean!) He had promised them he would return for the busy season.

He never called, never showed up, never contacted them, and they had no way to contact him. It was exactly the opposite of what he had told me about them giving us their blessings and him the okay to leave, in honor of his wedding. Poor guy just burned every bridge he crossed.

Each day I would find out more and more deceits that he had told about stupid things that he didn't even have to bring up; like telling me his mother was the first woman to ride a motorcycle from one end of South

America to the other. When I finally did speak to his mother, no, she had never done that (*but wasn't that story in some foreign film that came out?*) and she wasn't dying of cancer either, nor had she had any contact with him.

I no longer had any idea of whom exactly I fell in love with. Was his goodness that I saw yearning to manifest itself in him just smothered by the wretched, faithless, and manipulating serpent that slithered so gracefully into my life?

That's not true actually. It wasn't graceful.

It was explosive, like a hurricane ripping roots from their foundation, clearing a path through a forest of life, creating destruction where new growth would form soon after.

His suicide was shocking to many but when I look back at his words and actions, I think it was something he had been calculating for so long that he was on a course to self-destruction and didn't know how to back out of it. Maybe he didn't want to back out of it. He set himself up—perfectly.

I was the decoy to manifest the plan. I was the love that could keep him alive. It worked for thirteen months. I guess I wasn't strong enough to withhold the constant furor that his presence wreaked havoc on my stability. I gave in.

I realized that he had stripped me clean in so many ways. Physically, I had lost about 20 pounds and size 0's were hanging on my emaciated frame. I had also shed layers upon layers of skin from eczema that looked like someone had sprayed a load of acid all over my face, chest, arms and hands. I literally had open wounds that would itch and ooze as though all the toxins I had built up over hundreds of lifetimes were now literally seeping out through my pores.

It was frightening to look at me. The pity eyes appeared that much quicker. I looked horrid. It was questionable whether I would endure, or even survive. It was the frailest time in my life.

Mentally, emotionally and spiritually, he had been my cosmic goat/prod to make me move forward in my life, take care of myself, stand up for myself, and to stop letting myself be taken advantage of by those promising words of love and acceptance in exchange for the selling of myself.

Ok, years later, and I've hopefully gotten the hang of seeing these 'goat-prods' in my life. A couple of women over the years have stuck it to me, this goat prod process, but I definitely have a pattern with men, one that brings in those that nourish me and my soul for a while. Then, the shift happens, and the relationship is no longer healthful, and I allow them to harm me with disrespect, until I once again learn to stand up for myself, and say, "I'm done."

This learning curve is getting shorter and shorter… Oscar was 13 months, the last guy was 13 weeks. I'm improving in the process. Thirteen nanoseconds, that's the goal.

In my stronger, more compassionate moments, I could recognize the bigger picture of my time and relationship with Oscar. Nevertheless, I still had moments where I was caught up in the wreckage, not knowing where to begin to create order out of the chaos. My anger and hurt surfaced during those moments. How could I have stayed married to a man that was going to test my love and ability to forgive every single day, hour even, of my life?

It was an extreme relief to know I would no longer be under such pressure to constantly prove my love. Everything exhausted though his sieve-like heart, no matter how much was poured into it. Eventually, his heart would drain out and his emptiness would open the door for his demons.

He had a pathetic childhood. Who wouldn't be affected from being abandoned by their mother at 4-years-old? His abandonment issues mirrored my own. I thought we could work through them together. He helped me witness my patterns within this issue. I learned I abandoned myself more than others abandoned me.

I thank him for all those lessons and more. God bless him, hurricane that he was.

We actually were very pro-active with Tasha's schoolteachers, counselors and staff. We thought we were keeping up with the expectations of those people and professionals that were actually in her day-to-day life, and making sure Tasha was in as stable an environment as she could be. The school counselor even put together a "divorce class" for all the kids experiencing it in their family that semester. It was an incredibly pro-active program for the children. All of them found out they weren't the only one. Tasha found out she was lucky.

We made it a point to have her teachers for family night dinners, and to be very involved in her class and all her extra-curricular activities. I was leader of her Girl Scout Troop for several years (although I did take a hiatus after Oscar's death, for a while.) Like every Leader's daughter, we had times where she was proud and excited that I was leading, and then there were times when she wished it was another mom doing it. All in all, we had some really great times on our retreats and doing our projects. It was good medicine for me, too.

Even so, there were urgent pleadings from a couple family members, begging us to bring Tasha in to see a "special therapist," and get her the help she truly needed, because we obviously were blind to how poorly she was doing. There were many family and friends that were with Tasha on a consistent basis who supported our efforts and thought she was doing well, even without the circumstances. We figured these relatives saw her for the first time in months, and she was wild with excitement to be with all her cousins again (not to mention having had enough sugar to affect any tomboyish 8 year old…) But, we didn't want to be aloof to something we may not have been attuned to, after all. 'Squeaky wheels,' are somewhat like 'goat-prods' but don't physically hurt so much, except the ears and mind. Essentially, they meant to be helpful. It was done out of concern for Tasha, and that is always legitimate. They just didn't think we were doing right by her and she was suffering.

Synchronistically, which is always so easy to see in hindsight, we contacted the approved family therapist but she wasn't available for *six weeks*! Well, we decided it was worth the wait if she was as good as her recommendation. We explained our situation. The therapist thought things sounded well enough to hold off, but if we had any problems, we could contact her on an emergency basis.

There were no emergencies, until the suicide of course, which was precisely *six weeks* later. We went straight from the funeral service to the therapist's office for Tasha's long-awaited first appointment.

Angels were surely involved here, this was "Divine Timing" at its best.

Synchronicity is a newer term, not exactly psycho-babble, but more psychic-babble ;>) Really, it just means keeping your eyes and ears and heart and mind open to little nudges or feelings or memories that come out of nowhere. It could be a déjà vu kind of feeling. It's important to allow ourselves to witness these events, when you think of calling someone and the phone rings, and low and behold, it's them! This is more than sheer coincidence, as are many of those 'funny' moments.

We had been slightly upset that the therapist couldn't get us in before that six-week out appointment, but I was learning to let things go and see what happened with them, while still trying to be pro-active. Letting go of this one was the best thing I could do. I probably would have found another therapist whom I wouldn't have felt so good about, and wouldn't have gotten the 'approval', not that we really needed that, but…

Lee and I felt, before the suicide, that she was doing exceptionally well. She understood that we actually were doing what we promised her; staying family through the good, and the rough, times. This was Tasha's first encounter with the death of someone she cared for deeply and who was in her daily life, much less had made the decision to take his own life.

After the suicide, it was more difficult to gauge where Tasha was at, but we did our best to give her consistency *(even if we disagreed on what that meant, that itself was, at least, consistent.)* I felt it was important for all of us to take time to heal, and yet not get stuck in victimization of how hard life was for us. We started to do some charity work together on family nights, and it always helped us to remember how fortunate we are. We coped as best we could, easing each other's burdens. Thank goodness for 'service as therapy.' And, thank goodness for our wonderful therapist.

She was truly someone we connected with very well. After about six sessions between the three of us together and individually, she announced we had no more need to be in crisis counseling or any counseling, other than a particular issue here or there that might come up over the years.

She then actually offered, "Let me have your family's phone numbers, and I will call them directly and tell them how incredibly well Tasha is doing, with all the problems she's seen. You have dealt with her honestly and openly expressing your feelings and thoughts, even when she doesn't want to talk about the hard things because they make her or you cry. You've taught her that by talking through the hard issues, and crying through them, that you actually can get through them, and then over them."

We assured her that it wasn't necessary for her to call anyone. We were just happy she gave Tasha the thumbs up. As we left our last appointment, she suggested we write a book and share our story. She was one of the first to mention it, those six years ago.

There are those who still question what we allow Tasha to witness, but we feel it is our job to prepare her for the challenges life will undoubtedly offer her.

We often hear her give advice to her friends, and we beam from her natural emotional intelligence.

As our family has shifted into adolescence, it can still be a challenge for us to talk through the hard stuff. Those issues don't start out of nowhere, nor do they ever really end, they just shift and adjust to the conditions of circumstance we are experiencing at the time. Oscar, to his credit, taught me to laugh again after so many years of its suppression. His humor was much like Lee's mischievous nature. Oscar especially loved pranks.

Even from the other side, he'd been playing pranks on me; however, these were life threatening shenanigans. *I thought he was trying to see if I'd come with him. I would not.*

Nevertheless, I didn't know what to do when my car almost had a freak accident that surely would have killed me, had Lee not been there to help me. It's a long story… short of it, we were racing down the highway, I was pulling past him and he tried to get me to stop. I was laughing and thought he was acting freaked out that I was winning the race. I finally realized he was telling me to pull over, "NOW!" The rubber splashguard and inner rim of my front tire had somehow come off and wrapped itself around my axel, which was about to crack in half from the pressure and at 85mph,

I would have certainly crashed hard.

Then, I almost got electrocuted plugging in a TV. Lastly, I almost choked on a tiny piece of food out of nowhere. My Shaman friends, and a psychic, all warned me to get his ashes off my property, as soon as possible.

I took their warnings to heart, since things were getting a little bizarre. We did a ceremonial cleansing of the property.

Tasha and her friends placed seashells around the trees and yard as people gathered. A circle was made, and a picture of Oscar was set in the center. The entire property was smudged with sage smoke. The chanting began. A few of my friends (there to support me but not really into the ritual,) squeezed hands to help them suppress their laughter. My Shaman friends continued the ceremony, going through the motions; drumming, rattling… whooping and hollering, freeing his spirit to go forth, leave this world, and cheering him on to the next. Though the house did feel lighter, the fact remained that Oscar's ashes were still in the garage and he would continue to haunt me until I did something about it.

The problem was—I had promised him the month before he died, that I would take his ashes to the place we met and cast them into the ocean. We had been at a funeral of a father of a friend. We didn't even know the man, but I couldn't control my crying. Oscar said it was because I knew the next funeral we attended would be *one of our own.*

What? I really didn't believe him or want to go there, but looking back, it makes me realize that he was already planning on, waiting for, and manipulating the outcome for me to agree to divorce so he could kill himself already. He had to have a reason, like me throwing him out to give him permission to do so; it was almost as if his soul had a contract with my soul to come help me detach from my life I had created. When he was done, he could go back Home, but I had to *more than* separate. It was as though I had to willfully throw him out, so he had to push the envelope each day.

He actually got me to do it.

So could I resolve this dilemma of how to get his ashes to their pre-determined resting place? Into the Caribbean from Minneapolis? I had already sent half his ashes down to his family in Venezuela. He was specific about that. Half and half. He'd spent so much of my money that I didn't have the funds or the energy to return to our 'special place' to put him to rest, just yet.

As I was driving home one day, I crossed one of my favorite bridges in my neighborhood. It goes over Minnehaha Creek and there are beautiful weeping willows on either side of the street and on each side of the bridge. When I stopped to take it in and to take a breather, I visualized that the creek made it to the Mississippi River, which travels down to the Gulf and must eventually circle in to the Caribbean! Perfect!

Dilemma solved. I felt a bit guilty not following through exactly the way he made me promise him I would do it, but things were getting out of hand. I believed I had to get the ashes off my property, and fast.

So, here I was. It was a beautiful, windless day. It was so quiet that you could hear the water running over the rocks under the bridge. Everything was so calm and surreal. I made a prayer before releasing his ashes.

> *I love you but I release you from my life*
> *Thank you for all you have given me*
> *I forgive you for what you have taken*
> *May you be blessed with peace,*
> *And may you find forgiveness for me for not making the full journey*
> *(I suppose you're a higher being right now, so you can understand the*
> *   mundane problems that keep me from fulfilling my promise)*
> *May you travel to your resting place easily and swiftly.*
> *Goodbye, m'amor…*
> *   And, stop playing your tricks on me, OK?*

It was so perfect. Every color was shimmering off the reflection of the water and I felt like I was in some cosmic state of mind. I began to pour the ashes out of the container. I watched them fall into the water and rush, like a magnet, towards the sea.

Ashes of a cremated person are not what you expect them to be. I had already found this out when I separated them to send the other half to his family. There are pieces of bone, sometimes as big as your thumb, but there are plenty of ashes, too.

It was taking a very long time to pour them slowly and lovingly. After a while, I increased the angle to pour out the remaining contents. There was more than I realized and the container dumped out a huge heap to finish the job. At the very same moment, out of nowhere a gust of wind blew out and upward from under the bridge. Ashes flew *everywhere*! I was covered with his ashes!! *I was breathing them in*!!!

I screamed at him! "How could you do that to me? You jerk!"

I spat what felt like sand out of my mouth.

AAAGGGHHHH!

I just gave you a beautiful little ceremony, overcame all the latest lies I've uncovered, and I could have easily flushed you down the toilet, you shit! Are you having a good laugh?

Just had to have the last prank in there, huh?

Well, you've given me enough of them!!

I ran to my car and pulled out the wet wipes. (Ok, my daughter and her dad have always called me the 'wet wipe freak,' but let me tell you, I was never as glad as at that moment to have two fresh packs in my car.) I was fuming! I desperately wiped the ashes off my body, face and tongue. I couldn't do it fast enough.

"Yeah, well, back at you! Now your ashes are going to end up in the garbage and it's your own fault!" I yelled aloud.

Guilt overrode the anger. *How could I be so mean?* But, what about that prank? And the other pranks that almost killed me? I needed purification, big time.

I headed over to Lee's house, to my pool, *my mikvah* (the ceremonial purification practice in Judaism.) It's the biggest thing I miss about that house--if we're talking about 'things.' I built that pool as my saving grace, since the money would have been squandered on traveling the world, but I had gotten pregnant. I figured the water always soothed me, so if I couldn't travel the world, then I was going to make my world into my own little haven, pool included.

The chlorine would purify any death cooties, I was sure of it. *But, was I putting death cooties into the pool?* It was too late to ask. I dove under. I shook my head so the water would rinse away any residue in my hair. My hands could not scrub my body hard enough. *What if I missed some?* Lee and Tasha came out and joined me in the pool. I didn't think they were home. I didn't mention the ashes.

I felt like I was living the TV Movie of the Week, with my life playing out like a blockbuster, with heightened circumstances at every turn. It felt like everyone knew what was going on, or didn't know and wanted to know. I knew I needed to take care of myself. I needed to close this chapter of my life. I needed to settle back and just 'be' in my home. I needed to take the summer off. When Oscar died, any semblance of my life that I had built on the ruins of my marriage imploded.

When I found myself going into those moments of outrage, from injustice, or not wanting to see or deal with anyone and all the pain, I just wanted to hide. Just hide… I forced myself to reach back if there were people that reached out to me. I had seen enough depression and experienced enough in life to succumb to depression, but it just made me so angry to be victimized by life… I could not say, 'Why me? Why does this have to happen to me?' *I got myself here; there were red flags all along. I stayed.*

Those really difficult, lonely days that feel as if the world is out to get you, yeah, that's when I would go to sleep. I slept a lot. *I still use sleep as medicine. I like to sleep a lot… even though I don't get much!*

I had many dear good people that came to me and checked on me, that soothed me and supported me. Learning to accept help from people, learning to ask for help from people, those were huge lessons that were going on. I felt like I was in a surreal place. Maybe like a mockumentary horror flick, or some European psycho-drama with a twist of 'sick' in there. Suicide is not easy on the living.

I have had, for a long time, a sincere belief that everything we experience has been an opportunity for us to grow, to learn, to see something from another perspective. I think, and it is taught in many traditions, that our souls come to earth in physical form to experience and learn what the spirit cannot attain. Therefore, we are not here to hide from knowledge, but to seek knowledge. It is as though each life is a grade in school. Sometimes, we don't get the knowledge needed to move up, so we have to re-do the lessons. Now, as time moves faster, and we are living longer, *is it possible to re-incarnate in this life, in this body?*

To be re-born out of a womb that has nourished us in some way, but eventually is outgrown. The labor is painful, and we are literally wrenched, shoved, squeezed and thrown out of the life we just lived during gestation. *Could it be that each relationship is the gestation for the next? Can we love our relationships as the place where the seed of us is planted? Plants are continually outgrowing their pots if they are thriving, right?*

I didn't want to drown from this. I wanted to live, to be reborn without dying, to not have to live through re-learning everything, but to move forward consciously.

Death is sad, especially when it's someone who's so young. But who are we to say that's not exactly the amount of time that individual was supposed to be here?

My ability to focus and do something, other than wallow in my depression, was to get angry enough that I was not just going to survive this; I was going to thrive from this. And, that definitely was a piece of what kept me getting out of bed every day. People were going to talk about me. *Yep,* I thought, *then I'll give them something to talk about.*

It took me a long time to admit to Lee that I used his pool to wash the death cooties off. *Not very considerate of me, but funny.* Humor is another thing that got us through that year… Humor is one of the best medicine's you can give your body. A good laugh actually stimulates endorphin production and creates a euphoric feeling.

Thankfully, he laughed his head off at Oscar's last prank with the ashes. The pool only finished the story with a perfect *splash,* that I'm sure they both enjoyed.

Whew.

Lee - 6

Julie knew that I was always there for her if she needed me. I knew it meant a lot to her that I came to Oscar's funeral, which surprised many people. However, I didn't sit with Jules and Tasha. I sat with friends. I wanted to support her without crowding her in this trying time. I felt that me going to the funeral was important. I was showing respect for him, and Jules.

But mostly, for Tasha, who lost... someone close in her life. I've never been able to characterize him for Tasha and what he was to her but I know that she liked him and it did hurt her that he died. It was very tragic. I made sure that Tasha was taken care of, and we both helped Julie.

As for our family, the only relief was knowing that Julie was going to divorce him anyway. Julie was fragile and going through lots of inner turmoil. Knowing what I know today, and being tactless, it could not have ended better.

I hadn't wished him dead, but I remember thinking that the only way possible for Julie and me to have any kind of chance in our future was if something tragic happened to Oscar. That wasn't for at least a good couple... hours after the police took him. I'm just kidding, that wasn't right. I thought about it very fast. *What can I say? I'm being honest.*

We even had friends talking about it at his death even before his body was taken away, at the funeral, and still, at the Shiva. I was thinking, *here is yet another opportunity to put my family under one roof again.* I think that Julie needed a lot of friends around her, a lot of love around her. I knew that she still loved me as a friend, as a dear person in her life.

There were still many who hoped we would get back together. It wasn't just about what I wanted for us, but I also had hopes that those few relatives of Julie's (through this kind of tragedy,) would work harder to reconcile with her in some real way. Just to 'be there' throughout the hardship, sharing her burden. Some hopes die. At that point, there was no healing in that respect.

As hard as it was for me to understand, I was there for her Shaman gathering. I tried to help *'extricate Oscar's spirits from the house.'* I know there were many people that felt she was wacko, but it worked for her. It was something that Julie needed to be done for herself, and I had to respect that.

To me, a Shaman ceremony in your house is not that much different than a Shiva, in Judaism, or having a wake, in Christianity. Whatever works for the person, whatever makes that person feel better. I know Julie felt good about it and I was supportive as I could be the whole time.

Tasha was fond of Oscar. She liked him a lot. What is ironic is that I think she was one of the few people that didn't think at all about her mom and dad getting back together. She was the one who was okay with what her life was, how her life was. She had no problem with it. It was because of our honesty with her and our explaining to her about the divorce.

We had always reassured her, that as a family unit, we were still going to be together, be at family functions together and at school functions, take family vacations, continue having a family structure, just re-structured, and not living together. I think these were some of the reasons that she didn't have a need or a fantasy for her parents getting together.

Tasha kept being Tasha. The only thing that I believe changed for her was that she grew up faster. She saw things that opened her up to the world earlier. It made her a stronger person.

I was told that I was spoiling my little girl, that I was giving her everything she wanted, and that I was letting her run my life, by a lot of people. Remember, I didn't have this whirlwind, this whole other life that just started around me with another woman as Julie had with another man—you know, another pressure-filled, stress-filled environment.

I, too, was going through a difficult time, but mostly, trying to take care of Tasha, making sure that she was okay was my main concern. With everything that she had gone through, everything from me spoiling her to Julie getting re-married and his suicide, or familial dysfunction of being ostracized and not being included in a lot of extended family gatherings, many circumstances played into my 'spoiling' her. I wanted her to have some fun in life, too.

So, whatever she wanted to do for fun, we did! I wanted her to be happy with me and *want* to hang out with me. We shopped, a lot! It was so great to go shopping with someone who loved shopping. Julie always looked at it as a task to check off her list. She hated shopping. We went to miniature golf and roller bladed (which meant we had to go buy all the new equipment!) We biked (Tasha got a new one, and somehow I ended up with Oscar's hand-me-down, or I guess, inheritance?—but, it was a REALLY nice bike that I couldn't find anywhere to buy, so why spite myself, right?)

Tasha and I spent hours watching TV and movies together, playing board games or just doing our own thing while hanging out together, like reading magazines on the couch together. We loved our magazine time.

I also brought Tasha to my office with me frequently. I made her a name plate and she had her own little mini-office, with a mini-desk and chair set, pens and pads of paper, and a phone. She loved it. I loved her being with me.

We have always had a good time together. I had made her my focus in my life. You can call it spoiling her, but why not? Why shouldn't she have fun?

One of our best family-fun times is in the pool at my house. Julie had to fight with me about putting it in, another "NO" before I even thought about the 'positive potentiality' of the good family times that Jules knew it would provide. It was her way to cleanse her spirit, too. I watched her do that often.

Julie called me up and told me that she went to the creek and made a real nice ceremony for Oscar, and after, as she was emptying the container of his ashes into the creek, out of nowhere, a big gust of wind came and blew them right on her. It was sadly hysterical; I felt sorry for her. I just couldn't stop laughing so hard inside; it was just such a funny story. Here she is finally getting rid of him and he just doesn't want to leave her.

I didn't find out until much later that she had actually came and dove into my pool and cleansed herself of the ashes, which I also found very, very funny. In fact, it explains something very odd that happens at my house daily. Every single day there is a phone in my kitchen that rings twice between 8:15 and 8:30 pm, the time I was giving him mouth-to-mouth resuscitation! It's the only phone in the house that does it. No one is ever on the other end if we pick it up, and there's never any called ID showing up. So, she washed his ashes in my pool, and now he's around here somewhere. Every time I hear that phone ring, I say, "There's Oscar calling." *Almost all our friends have witnessed this phenomenon.*

As close as friends that we were in our marriage, we have become in some ways even closer now. I have become more honest with her, although sometimes it still takes me awhile. When we need a shoulder to cry on, we turn to each other. Some people say that we are still friends, or friendly, only because of our daughter and that if Oscar was still alive, we would not be as close. Maybe so, but I choose to believe that we would be this close, as the psychic said, "Deep, deep foundation."

Tasha – 6

Why did he kill himself???

Once upon a time, there lived two very different people, one, a girl who had lived in Minnesota her whole life, but who loved to travel, and who always solved problems. That girl is Julie Rappaport. The other person is a man who was born in Venezuela and moved to the Cayman Islands. He loved to sail his boat, loved to have a good time, but there was one bad thing... HE LIED. This man's name was Oscar. No one really suspected that he lied except for my mom. I don't know how she could tell, but she just could. She said his eyes would change colors or something like that, but she didn't even know about it at first.

My mom went on a trip to the Cayman Island with her friend. They decided to go on a sailboat for the afternoon. That's when my mom met Oscar. I guess they fell in love, or something. He decided to move to Minnesota, and my mom said he could come live with us. He got a job of painting sailboats and cleaning them. He took us sailing, too, but lake sailing is very different than ocean sailing.

Well, soon after that they decided to get married. It was a small wedding at the house and very pretty. I got to be the flower girl!

Once, my mom called into his work to see when he was coming home. They had said he had left the job about a month ago and went to a different shop. My mom got furious. That night when he came home, all I remember was screaming, lots and lots of screaming.

Oscar was a person you could love one second and then hate the next. He was very confusing. I remember him always making me and my friends laugh and have a good time, like kids do. But, then again, I also remember him yelling and screaming and that just scared me. I guess he was just a different kind of person at different times.

My mom became friends with Oscar's ex-wife down in Venezuela. I became friends with his son. I never met them but I saw pictures of them and that was cool. I guess I wouldn't picture Oscar as a dad. I mean, after he died, we found out he had had sex with another woman and also had a little girl. He never met her. She never met him. He didn't even know about her. That also made me think very differently about Oscar.

Well, you would never know if Oscar was telling the truth or not but, like I was saying, my mom knew when he was lying. I didn't find this out until after he died but I guess that didn't really matter. All I knew is that my mom couldn't ever trust Oscar like she thought she could.

My mom told me that Oscar was really depressed, so I tried to make him happy. I made him pictures, I tried to play games with him but I guess that didn't really work. I miss him very much but then again I think if he is in heaven, then he is definitely in a better place where he can enjoy himself much more.

On April 23rd, around 8:15 at night, we received a phone call from my mom's house. All I remember was my mom screaming and it was very shocking. I said, "Mom, are you okay?"

"Yes, Pumpkin, give the phone to Daddy, everything is okay." Then I gave the phone to my dad. Once he hung up, he made me pack a suitcase with clothes and took me over to my neighbor's house. My dad whispered something into my neighbor's ear as I went off to go play with my friend. Then my dad left.

I was just hanging around at my friend's house and stayed until about 11:00 p.m. at night. My dad came and picked me up. Once I got home, I asked what happened. He told me Mommy got locked out of her house and started panicking, so, everything was okay and I went to bed as though nothing was wrong.

The next morning though, I woke up and my mom and dad were there. They kept me home from school that day. They made me breakfast and then they told me, "Sweet pea, Oscar committed suicide."

I was in total shock. I didn't really know how to react. I didn't know if I was sad, no emotions came to me. All that came out was,

"Oh my gosh."

They said that Mom got home and saw Oscar's car in the garage. It was very smoky in there. She went to see what happened, she opened the door and a dead body of Oscar came out. My mom called my dad's house and then that's what happened. My dad said he called the police and everyone came, so a lot of people were there with my mom. Oscar left a message on my mom's phone. He said not to tell his son. He was very sorry to do this but he couldn't stand living. My mom said that they were going to separate. I started to cry. We had a very nice and quiet funeral.

We had Oscar cremated and sent down to Venezuela. My mom took some of his cremation and threw it in the river. It was her own quiet ceremony.

Oscar has taught me, that if you lie or do something bad or good and aren't honest with your loved ones, you never know how or what might happen. It taught me to tell the truth and be open with my parents. I miss him dearly, but it was his choice. I know he's probably happier now.

The end

CHAPTER 6 DISCUSSION
Recognizing Perceived Endings

There is a concept found in many traditional texts that says, "*Suffering is caused by ignorance of the fact that all things will change.*"

When we are ignorant of that fact, we hope and expect things to stay the same. When things inevitably do change, clutching at '*what was*' causes suffering as we grip the womb. Resisting birth causes pain for both the life-giver (relationship) and the gestate (participants.)

What we find we are willing to do, in order to have that 'love of a lifetime,' is often different than when we are willing to concede in the throws of losing it. Again, our concessions are also different than after a time of recuperation from having lost that love. Perhaps we are one of the lucky ones, who have never experienced being the one who feels dumped.

Being 'In Love' is different from a deep and lasting love; I think 'In Love' is a drug, an addiction—there is that euphoric feeling that any problems can be resolved because this 'true love' is so strong. I also believe that when we're 'In Love,' we fear not being in love, as well as not being loved back. We fear them loving someone else more. We fear a lot when we're in love--that we might lose that drug.

I read a great piece about 'in love high's' being doled out so delightfully like a drug dealer handing out fresh cheap, or not so cheap, free drugs, getting one hooked and then you start having to pay for it. In paying for it, that's when we start to give ourselves away.

"Okay, I'll do this to make you happy and love me...Okay, I won't do that anymore if it makes you unhappy or not love me...Okay..."

Eventually, we might ask, who are we then, after having given ourselves away or taken on other personas that perhaps are not our own?

Love does not instill fear in, nor take power from, anyone or thing. True love empowers.

When we no longer fit into the world we've created, or that world has some catastrophe, we begin to look at either how we can fit in again, avoid it all together, or create the world we want. We begin to reflect on what we have done or not done and begin to 'come true' to ourselves as other than that which we have fantasized ourselves to be. We make drastic changes and small changes, or perhaps no changes at all, but the fact is our lives have changed whether for better or worse.

<u>Evocations:</u>

1. What have endings in our life taught us? Have they empowered us or dis-empowered us?

2. Do I choose to allow endings to propel me towards an inspiring future or keep me stuck in the past?

3. Do I witness the power of my own thoughts and words? Can I witness my use of them to gain power, or give power in exchange for love?

4. What would I do if a relationship doesn't last, for whatever reason? How would I survive? What would define me without this relationship?

5. Am I able to deal with my child learning things outside of what I want them to learn? Do I protect them from hardships, or help them deal with life's challenges?

6. Do I love myself? What do I need to be, in order to get me to love me the way I wish someone else would love me?

7. What helps me get out of bed on those days when being under a rock isn't enough to relieve the suffering or feelings of being overwhelmed?

CHAPTER SEVEN

Discarding Old Blueprints, Re-Creating the Structure

Lee - 7

Many times, I told Julie that her concerns about our sexuality were "all in *your* head." It turned out they weren't in *her* head all those years. She used to ask me to go see a doctor. "*There's nothing wrong with a man, a man is a man,*" I'd say. I just would not have the energy to give her what she wanted—even though I knew that she was so in love with me and devoted to me, and that she wanted only me.

Night after night after night, it would be like time just ticking. It got to a point, after so many years, where I was embarrassed to go see a doctor. I had a luscious woman in my house, in my bed, and I couldn't get myself to jump her. Even after I knew she had an affair with whomever, and after we split, even when Oscar came here and after he passed away, even after some other guys she dated, it didn't make me go see a doctor. There was too much else going on. What was the point? Why bother?

Most of the dates I had gone on in the beginning, and even now, most were like... like Julie and I lying in bed all those years, and she would talk me to sleep. That's what the dates were like, conversations so shallow that they didn't even notice my eyes crossing, giving out nothing. It might not have been the person. It might have been me. Well, then, it just wasn't what I was looking for.

A cute girl in Las Vegas who I would see at the tradeshows over the last five years or so, came up to me and told me she had noticed me for a few years. She wanted to know if we could, "*get together for dinner.*" I told her I was flattered but leaving for home that night. She asked where home was, and when I told her Minneapolis, she perked up and said, "I'm going to be there next weekend to visit some friends. Do you mind if I call you?"

I told her it was no problem and handed her my card. After years of looking at her, the minute I started talking to her, I got turned off. It seemed like it was a routine for her... "I've noticed you... can I have your number..." They were pick-up lines! She looked so beautiful from 30 feet away.

I do know that I don't want to go out and have some girl agree with everything I say, or not be who she really is just to impress me or please me. Even though I was acting that way, trying to please and be what she wanted. It's not that people have to talk about being evolved, and I don't mean to be judgmental, but I'm not going to be blinded just to be with someone else. I will not do that. Since Julie and I split up, I've started to really like myself. I'm not going to compromise myself. If they can't be who they really are around me, than forget it.

It's good not to mince words around me. You don't have to be intimidated by me. But, as for dating, what about it? CHECK, please!

It wasn't until a new guy came on the scene as Julie's new beau that finally something in me said, "Okay, that's enough."

I admit I still felt cheated on to some degree, even if I told her to go date other men. I probably did go to a doctor because I still had visions, fantasies that one day Julie would want to come back to me. *Why I didn't do it during our marriage, who knows?*

It goes back to not knowing what you're going to miss until you don't have it anymore. Consciously or subconsciously, Julie, by going ahead and living her life, was the one that was able to get me off my ass and go see a doctor. I was able to get angry enough, even though we weren't married, to go see a physician. *I should have gotten angrier while we were still married, but I didn't.*

Finding out about my condition, my pituitary tumor, alone at my house, talking to my doctor, seeing it; it was pretty terrifying. I was traumatized. I didn't want to listen to him. All I heard was, "... tumor in the brain..." I called my 'doctor' friend, Julie Rappaport, the first person I told about it. It was hard to tell her because I really didn't have a lot of the facts. She immediately got on the internet and did one of those 'all-nighters' she's known for when she is seriously working on something. She looked into every possible detail of what this kind of tumor was. She literally put her life on hold those few months of pre-Mayo and post-Mayo.

She did everything with me, and for me, during that period. From making doctor's appointments, going with me to all the doctors', spending time with me down at the Mayo Clinic, waiting for three, four hours during blood tests, MRI's, you name it.

Once the medication took effect, and the pituitary tumor went down, I had more of the right hormone levels in me. It was natural for me to have more 'manly' feelings. *They suddenly came out of nowhere.*

I always thought it was easier **not** to deal with something. Don't say anything about it, hope it will go away. That's the way I was, though I've learned dealing with it makes things easier. You don't have to deal with it all the time once you've dealt with it. *As time has gone by, I have opened up to a few people, but I'm still kind of reserved in who I talk to and what I talk to them about.*

Even though my sexuality is in a much stronger place right now in terms of the want for it, it is still not where it needs to be. Physically it is all there, but mentally there are still some scars from my marriage that need to be worked on. There is no question about that. I was able to find out more about myself in a 2 ½ year period after my divorce, than I did in the 17 years I was married. *Two years after the divorce I finally found the cause of my lack of interest: a pituitary tumor, but by then it was too late to erase the last couple years..., decades...*

Julie

If you're not going to communicate, whether consciously or subconsciously, with someone--than realize the effect is "mis-communication," which leads to assumptions. Our thoughts and words spring forth into action (which could actually be no action,) which in turn grow into habits and root into character. If we can begin to witness how we think, than we have the opportunities to correct our thoughts to more positive and compassionate thoughts.

This is a conscious effort, and does not evolve without the pain of witnessing our own structures in which we imprison ourselves. But it is truthful that the harder we resist learning the lessons of our lives, the harder they have to be to break through our skulls and into our hearts. We each have choices at each and every moment of how to act or react. When we allow our selves to witness, we begin to see our patterns and eventually learn how to circumvent them prior to their occurrences.

Tasha did witness me breaking down a few different times, none of which I was proud of. If she would retract a hug, or pull back and say something unkind--as daughters and mothers can do to each other--I would react in kind, which was not very kind. I knew I did my own share to my own mother, and here was my karma, as she prophesized, "Just you wait…" But Tasha and I were already breaking the mould I was so afraid of repeating. Our tickle time was definitely one of the best things we did together almost every night. She needs to release the energy she pulls in and uses all day, and if we missed tickle time, there was sure to be a tantrum in its stead. But we grew to witness that need and pattern, so we used it… like biofeedback.

Sometimes, when we are very vulnerable, we don't have the strength to keep ourselves from lashing back. I did not want to be that kind of parent. I would always make a point afterwards to sit with Tasha and talk, apologizing for throwing my built-up energy at her. We would actually be able to bond afterwards, and I think it had just about everything to do with my acknowledging that I had lost it. *That wasn't what I wanted to teach her, and yet, she will face it in others as well as herself as she lives and I do want to teach her to look at it when it happens, make amends for it if needed, and to use it to help communicate better.*

One of Lee's greatest regrets was not what he did do, for he did do so much for us over the years. But, he has held regrets for what he didn't do. Many people have told me the same rings true in their own lives.

What fears hold us back from doing something we know we should, and what fears keep us running from what we need to face?

For me, the fear of dying and not having lived true to my nature was scarier than the thought of dying having lived true to myself. So, death, something I was already accustomed to and somewhat comfortable with, was not my fearful motivating force. One motivating force for me is to consider how I would tell God I enjoyed living when I was the one making my life's decisions that were keeping me from my joyous nature.

There is the story of the old devotee, who in times of a great flood refused help from his neighbors, three separate times before being consumed by the flood. When he reached God, he asked why he, such a devotee, was not spared from the flood. He was upset that in his devout practice, God had not saved him. God's reply was, "I gave you three opportunities, only you can choose to use them when I present them to you."

I guess I was putting it out to God that I was ready to have a relationship again, because I was getting all these phone calls, "There's a nice guy that would like to meet and settle down with a nice Jewish girl!"

Here I was, a divorced widow, and I was about to go back out onto the market? My response? "Wowww! Well, tell him good luck!" I wasn't available.

I'm not going to be settling down again. I've done that twice, given myself away, *literally*. I left one marriage of eggshells and walked into another marriage of eggshells.

The night of Oscar's death, I pretty much cracked in half watching Lee try to resuscitate him. Lee did mature that night, in front of both of us. We both watched the hurricane leave our fortress. We were still standing, with Tasha, as a family.

All of the sudden, Lee was willing to go to new restaurants, willing to travel, willing to go and do different things. What had evolved was that Lee was willing to recognize me as me, being that friend to me that he hadn't been. If I was having financial difficulties, he wanted to help. It was really nice, but I started to feel awkward about the whole thing. Even though I know he had all good intentions of helping me out, and kept announcing that it was because I was Tasha's mom, it felt like he thought maybe this was another way for us to get back together. Finally, a year after Oscar's death, I asked Lee about it and found it was still a taboo subject.

Tasha bounced the basketball to me and ran off to climb the tree. Lee went to tend to the fire pit, which seemed to have gone down to a smother of smoke. We just finished a family-friendly game of H-O-R-S-E. Lee and I were together all the time and got along so great over the last year. Maybe we were ready to make our relationship work. We hugged and were affectionate, but it was still a 'kin-type' of affinity.

Tentatively, I asked, "What's going on with us? Everyone seems to just be waiting for us to get our heads together and be a couple again."

Lee stabbed at the fire and more smoke issued out. "What's the question? Who cares what others think? Are you happy the way things are? We're best friends, that's all. There's nothing weird about our relationship.

You want more from it?"

I said, "I don't know… Can I ask if you've done anything about your sexuality?" Lee picked up his drink up, but it tipped and doused the fire. The coals hissed. "If you want sex, go get it. We're great the way we are…"

Well, that answered that. I was trying to figure out what was going on with us, and in that sense, our relationship had not changed.

Okay.

I was now open and willing to a relationship with someone, and yet I was wary of what that exactly meant. I never lived without a man in my life until now. Since Oscar died, I have had a few different men enter my life. Nice as they are, I'm just not there. I really like having my own house, bed, habits, idiosyncrasies…

But, I did try to have a relationship with a particular man that summer. He was a dark, thin, rugged, handsome Jewish man who arrived on his motorcycle. He was a little bit off beat like me, a little rough around the edges, but he possessed a real finesse. We spoke about philosophy, life, the cosmos and how energy exchanges…

We sat by my outdoor fire pit together on one lovely evening. Lights were strung around the yard and it felt magical. I crossed my leg over his and he ran his hand along my thigh. The fire spewed its sparks into the air. We both laughed. My phone rang. I apologetically picked up, but I could see it was Tasha, "Hi, Sweetpea."

Lee's voice came through the line, "Hey, can we come by and say goodnight?" Caught, I said, "It's not really a good time…" I could tell he was bummed, "Fine."

Early the next morning he called again to see if they could stop by to say good morning. This time, he got angry. "We can't see Mommy right now, because she still has a man in her bed! Sorry, baby." CLICK. I looked at the phone in horror. I couldn't believe he just did that to her. We got past it, he apologized to both of us after realizing the damage it did, and that no good came from it.

A few weeks later, I was sitting at my computer, in the dark of my little hovel off my master bathroom. I had created an office in there, where you couldn't really stand, but I didn't need that. I would duck in and slide right into my chair that was surrounded by three tabletop desks, all piled with various loads of work.

The phone rang, and I was hesitant to pick up, as I had just sunk my teeth into my work and had planned an 'all-nighter' ahead. I didn't want to be bothered just then, but it was late and I saw that the caller ID showed it was Lee. I thought I'd better pick up. Maybe Tasha was sick at this late hour.

Lee's voice was shaky. "I have to tell you something I've needed to tell you for a while... I've got a problem..."

I laughed, and said, "You've got more than one problem, honey..." But, I realized he was not laughing. He started crying profusely. His words were jumbled, but "...TUMOR" was all I heard.

"WHAT?! Wait, wait, wait, back up and speak slowly..."

Lee stopped, and took a couple of breaths. "I'm so sorry, you were right all along... I have a tumor in my head, and it's the reason I don't have a sex drive... I almost couldn't tell you... Look what I've done to our family!" *It feels like SHIT to have been right about this!* He told me that what he had was called a 'pro-lac-ti-no-ma...'

This became my only focus. Hours passed on the clock and light began to seep in. Birds were chirping, and I had not only several papers with different notes, but also printed articles, names of doctors in the area, pictures of the tumor... By the time full daylight arrived, I had organized the piles and called Lee. He didn't sleep either. He cried into the phone, "I can't stop living the years of our marriage, how it ended...God, Boo...I'm so sorry."

Together we visited several doctors' offices, each showing us charts and diagrams, selling themselves and their specialty. We became more and more frustrated, and less and less confident of the medical system. The last surgeon we spoke to before going to Mayo Clinic was 'Dr. Mal,' an athletic, 50-ish guy who had hung pictures on the walls of himself in front of his chalet in Aspen. He irritated us both. He was quick to point out the faults of the other surgeons we saw, and why he was better than they were for the job. Lee and I agreed he could definitely sell swampland to poor folk.

"What? You're going to get an opinion at Mayo Clinic?! They're a bunch of communists down there! They have no incentive to do your surgery at all. Don't waste your time."

Wow. What an ass!

His incentive seemed to be to pay for the mortgage on his ski chalet.

Then, finally at Mayo Clinic, we meet "Dr. Good." He calmed us instantly.

"Now, Lee, I do surgery because I love to do it. I don't get paid any more or any less if I do it or not. And yours, well, it's a challenging one since it's right next to the carotid artery... the artery that supplies the brain with blood..."

We were blown away. None of the other five surgeons mentioned that. They all said it was an easy, quick shot! The doctor continued, "My question to Lee is, why would you want a surgery that carries more of a risk of damaging good tissue when all you have to do is take a pill that will shrink the tumor and make everything better in no time? There are side effects, but there is no recovery time."

Lee responded, "I have absolutely no good reason, now that I have good, straight facts." *It's amazing what a business surgery and medicine are.* In finishing my degree, I had to take History of Medicine. I thought, *Oh, great, someone to convince me for four months how wonderful the AMA is... blech.* Instead, I was shocked each class when everyone was walking out while I was waiting for the last words of the lecture. This professor explained the 'business of medicine' as part of the history. It's been quite a monopoly these last 80 years.

It turns out, the doctors at Mayo told us that estimates of *over 25% of the men in this country are walking around with the same tumor!* **That is why Viagra is the top selling drug.** No one needs to take a blood test in order to get a prescription. More commission is made off Viagra than off the prolactinoma medication, which is outrageously priced. **A simple blood test will alert your doctor that you may have a curable disease,** rather than symptoms that are simply masked or poo-poo'd off by the dealer, I mean, doctor. *Whoops. I know, it's all legal and tested by the government.* The only problem is that you might have to know enough to ask your doctor to give you a blood test for it.

This alone might save several marriages!

Two weeks after he started taking the medicine, Lee and I were bike riding. We were on a particularly bumpy patch when an older, heavier woman bent over to pick something up. Lee got a "woo-hoo" look on his face, looked down at his crotch, looked at her and smiled like a teenager. I started laughing. "Oh, is the medicine kicking in? Welcome to adolescence!"

Lee's eyes sparkled with knowing, and then filled up with tears. "I don't know if I should jump for joy or punish myself the rest of my life for what I've done to you and us..."

I walked over to him, put my arms around him, kissed his cheek and rubbed his back. He delighted and then depressed. He said, "Just being touched has a whole different sensation throughout my whole body."

Lee's condition, Lee's unfolding, reminds me of a story.

I was walking down the street one day, looking side to side, noticing all the things there were to see, and all of the sudden, I fell into a hole. I hadn't looked where I was going, and didn't see that there was a hole there. I was so angry.
WHO PUT THAT HOLE THERE? How dare they!?

What's the matter with the city? How can they have such a dangerous thing left out in the open? I tried to get out of this hole. It was just impossible. My hands were aching from trying to pull myself up and not being able to find a hold to get myself out of this hole.

My anger grew. Each time I fell back down, depression set in a bit more because I couldn't get out. At a certain point, I just lied down surrendered and wept. I asked, "Why me, why did this have to happen to me? Everything was going just fine! Why is the universe treating me so badly?"

Then, dawn came and there was a bit of light that reflected on a stone and, then another stone. I saw a path there I hadn't seen before. There were almost actual steps to get myself out. How did I not see them before?

Weary as I was, I made the attempt and came out of that hole. I was so happy to be out of that hole. It was so marvelous to be out. But, I was angry still, that there was a hole there. I tried telling people about it. They just nodded, and said, "Yep, there's a hole there." Nobody did anything about it. Frustrated, I threw my hands up and walked away.

The next day, I was walking down that same street. At the beginning of the street, I remembered that I was there yesterday. It was such a horrible experience. I had to remember, even though I would have rather forgotten the whole incident.

I continued walking, cautiously, but became distracted by something and BOOM! I was back in the hole again! Damnit! If it wasn't for that distraction, I wouldn't be here again! *How could I have let this happen to myself again?! But, it wasn't my fault! It shouldn't have been there! Someone should have done something about that damn hole I was in!*

Anger spewed out at the distraction, at the city, at the people around that weren't there to help, that didn't help, and that just kept walking by. I couldn't get out again.

Somehow, I remembered, oh yeah, there were steps. Where were those stones I was able to use? But it was dark. I couldn't find them right away. Eventually, I was able to find one of them. Just being able to hold on to it helped me to remember that I did it once before and, I can get out of this place, again.

I walked away, grateful that I had been able to save myself. Grateful that I had been able to find the perseverance within myself to not give up, to not sink and wallow in a depressed state at the bottom of that hole. No one was going to help. I had to do it myself. And, I did.

It was so much easier for me to blame others for my walking into that hole, not once-but twice.

Who wants to admit what *we get ourselves into?*

How many of us can relate to those holes that we fall into in our lives, or that we find blame for others for the fact that we have fallen back down into this hole? When do we come to a place where we recognize it's up to us to figure out how to pull ourselves up? Occasionally, we'll throw out a "Help!" instead of a cry of rage, and once in a while, that call for help will be heard and help will be offered. But, if we don't attempt to help ourselves to get up and out of these holes, if we only expect to be saved from them by others, then we might just end up living our life in that hole.

It all goes back to insecurities. There's something in life that makes us think that if we don't talk about something, it will go away. In reality, the only way we can move past it is to go through it. You can't go over, under or around it; you must go through it. Many of us were brought up to believe that if we just avoid it, it will go away, even though every experience we have is giving us the contrary message to that.

I had come to a place in my life where I felt I would rather die trying to get out of that hole and back into living, with all of the challenges and holes I might fall into otherwise, than to just stay in that hole, stay under a rock, or just keep running, similar to wandering. However, wandering doesn't necessarily mean you are running from something, it just means you are willing to take on all the sights that there are to behold. *Moreover, that you are willing to let yourself trip and fall.*

Tasha - 7

The differences between my parents are actually pretty good, they give me a balance. My mom doesn't like shopping but my dad does. I have always enjoyed shopping. I occasionally have had good shopping experiences with my mom, but I had to get my homework done first.

With my dad, it's good because I feel freer but I also know that I am not reading or getting my education up to the level that I want it to be. *I now realize that I have to do that, even if he doesn't tell me to.* I've always liked my mom for teaching me that.

Sometimes I do see that my mom will be disappointed in my dad's decisions for me. My dad will be kind of like, "Oh, I'll let you do this, don't worry about your mom, she's just having one of those nights." However, usually they do support each other and talk about things before they make their final decision on the big stuff.

I know that my parents do have a little bit in common when it comes to making decisions. For example, at the beginning of the divorce they thought two weeks at each of their houses would be good. As I grew older, of course, I started to need to shop more and get more clothes. I felt as though I needed a longer time span so it wouldn't be so much energy moving all my clothes there, and back. I also wanted to be with my parents for a longer period of time. We decided, well I decided, it would be better if we do it for one month at a time.

The first week you move and make everything how you like it. The second week you are just starting to be familiar with staying there and getting into their routine. Then, the third week you're actually enjoying them and you love being with them and you have the jokes together and all, but by the fourth week, you're like, *Get me the heck out of here!*

At least now, all of us make most of the decisions together. We definitely have that open communication. Everything seems to have worked out for the better.

CHAPTER 7 DISCUSSION

Recognizing Healing

Circumstances that life offers, to strengthen our resilience and fortitude, can often knock us off balance. They might put us into a situation where we may have judged another, declaring we would *never* break such a standard rule of conduct. We all have our rationalizations of how we can break our own rules that no one else is allowed to break. We can claim that the circumstances 'made me do it.' Do we allow the one we judge the same circumstances we allow ourselves in breaking those rules?

This double standard of judgment is a difficult gate to pass through in self-actualization. In studying the laws of Karma, we understand that we create our future by what we put into the present or have put into the past. The more we are aware of Karma in our lives, the quicker it plays itself out.

In a sense, by being loving to others, even when they are despicable, we are being loving to ourselves--by not setting ourselves up to have to experience what we are judging the other for choosing in their circumstances, that made them so despicable. I'd rather have the compassion for them, than have to set myself up to be in their shoes.

Somehow, love has gotten mixed up in its theme that is played out, and I still say, all our fears come down to a basic fear of not being loved, lovable, or loving enough to have that elusive 'end-all, be-all' love in our lives. We will do anything to get it, for what is being sold as love, it seems, is worth our souls. But is this love?

In being loving to others, there is often the conflict of being loving to one's self. More often for women, a decision has to be made whether to give the self away in order to love another on a higher level than ourselves, or perhaps our life, itself. Is this a subservient love, as a worshipper to an idol?

We might make new vows to ourselves, promising never to leave our self. This does not mean never allowing love to enter our lives again. But how can we love others truly if love does not emit from the inside out? When we say we cannot live without someone, that we *need* them in order to be whole, what does this mean? How did we live before we met them? How have billions of people lived having lost their loves, whether to another or to time... I say, the possession piece is similar to idolatry, and is a manifestation of ego rather than compassion and empowerment.

Listen to the words of most love songs out there. They all have to do with giving our selves away or belonging to another rather than, as Whitney Houston made famous, "Learning to love yourself is the greatest love of all".

This 'love of self' is where we can find love for those whom have hurt us, or that we have hurt. This is where gratitude and responsibility overcome victimhood, blame, and shame.

A snowstorm froze and covered my beautiful garden. Thankfully, I had already tended to it, and assured myself that come spring, it would be in full bloom once again, with all its vibrant colors and perfumes. Clearly, life continues when even what seemed devastation has occurred. *What have I learned from the precious seasons?*

If we can look at our souls as our own garden, plant seedlings we want to cultivate, tend to them with loving care, prune and weed what stunts their growth, and offer its harvest to those in need. This is what the seasons begin to teach, that for everything there is a time and a season, even relationships.

Evocations:

1. How do I love myself? Does that conflict with being loving to others?
2. When I am mourning from a loss, do I sabotage myself/others? Or do I make a conscious effort to treat myself lovingly?
3. Do my actions bring long-term healing or short-term bandaging?
4. Do I accept responsibility for hurtful actions or words and apologize sincerely? Do my actions corrupt my words believability?
5. Do I dwell in victimhood, always blaming others for my misfortunes?
6. Do I protect myself from hardships, or deal with life's challenges?
7. Do I appreciate what I've got, while I have it? Do I dwell on what I have lost when it is gone?
8. How would I re-create my life if there were nothing holding it back? What would I need to release in order to attain that life?

CHAPTER EIGHT

Re-Incarnating in This Life,
Preparing to Launch

Julie

All my growing up years, my formative years, I had watched my mother be only hindered by a man. So, to hear her say, after my stepfather passed away, "I'm nothing without a man" was so confusing and irritating to the core. At a young age, I made the decision that I would never be 'nothing' without a man in my life.

Funny, how things work out.

I had always known that I loved Lee. I had always thought that I could live without him, or anyone for that matter, because I lived through death so many times in my life. I learned you could learn to live without someone in your life. That life does go on.

Still, I had one surprising day, where I could not get a hold of Lee. I was very, very worried about him. I went into a panic. The panic was, *what would I do if something did happen to him?* The revelation that I could go to that kind of desperate place was a shock to me, that I could let someone mean so much to me, that Lee meant so much to me.

When I think back on my marriage to Oscar, I'm sure it was upsetting to him that I cared about Lee so much. I remember one conversation when Oscar had asked me where we would be buried together. The look on my face must have revealed my feelings and thoughts, as I answered, "Oh, I will probably be cremated." I wasn't a very good liar, didn't have a very good poker face… What I was really thinking was, *I never thought about not being buried next to Lee!* I'm sure that was wounding, even though that was my least intention. Oscar knew I didn't want to hurt him, or anyone. I did love him, too.

At one point after Lee's Mayo stint, I got very sick. I sent Tasha and the dog over to Lee's house to spend the night. The next night, I ended up staying overnight in the hospital, having been diagnosed with pneumonia. I really did think I was going to die there for a while. I had plenty of time to lie in bed and think about all those things that you think about before you are going to die. *Who would care?* It was interesting.

I got home from the hospital, and God bless Lee. He was trying to do what was right. He was trying to make me feel comfortable being home.

But, you know, when you need to recuperate, you just need to sleep. Lee wanted Tasha to come watch over me after school. Then, he planned on coming to my house and staying overnight on the couch, so he could watch over all of us.

I told Lee that it would be easier on me if he would take Tasha and the dog home with him and just let me rest. He wouldn't hear of it. He was going to make dinner and clean my house and put her to bed. He even brought a movie for us to watch and a book for me, so I could just escape.

What I really should have done was to have gone upstairs and gone to bed, but it was a family night and I really was not that tired. "Okay," I thought, "I'll read the cheesy, passionate book-of-the-month." (You know the kind, 'his hand runs up her body, searing with passionate...' blah, blah, and blah. I wasn't really in the mood for a rendezvous after the last couple of days of hospital hair, but... those writers are good!)

I told Lee, "If you are going to stay overnight, you don't have to sleep on the couch. Remember how we stayed in the same bed down in Mayo before your MRI?"

I had just held him that night in Mayo. We were both so scared. It still was so reassuring to know that, even though we weren't comfortably sleeping, we were there as a comfort to one another. As for this night, in my bed, I think it made him feel better to think I needed his help, which was sweet but wasn't necessary. Sleep was necessary.

But this night, he responded to me by saying, "You know, that night... I wanted to have an urge. I wanted to have a desire for you so much, but I just didn't. I was trying to will myself to do it. Tonight I know that you are sick, and it's totally inappropriate for me to have an urge to be with you, but I have a hard on that won't go away."

It felt good that we could talk about him having the desire to be intimate at all, but I was adamant that I was sick and on prescription drugs that were making me hallucinate, which he understood. We shared the bed, but we were NOT going to have sex.

Instead, we lay in bed talking, like old times, and laughing, but I was also hallucinating. The sound of the baby monitor (I still kept up in my bedroom, in case Tasha needed me,) was driving me crazy with its constant static. I felt like the whole room was electrified and it seemed like every spirit I'd ever known was waiting to see if we were going to consummate once again.

In my whirling state from the painkillers, I actually saw Oscar in front of me, in front of our bed together that I was lying in with Lee. Oscar's hand was in my face shaking, waving, "SEE ME!! Don't do this!!!"

But, in my hallucination, it felt like the rest of the crowd of spirits were yelling, "DO IT!! DO IT!!"

I yelled at them all, "STOP! I WILL MAKE MY OWN DECISION HERE! I HAVE FRIGGIN PNEUMONIA! LEAVE ME ALONE!"

Lee was a little freaked out by this outburst, but he also noticed that the monitor did stop buzzing. I told him I couldn't have sex with him again. He said he didn't ask to have sex with me. I could tell he was confused, yet, for the first time, he was willing to discuss our intimacy. He said he knew how I felt about him exploring his sexuality without me but that he thought, on the flip side, that I was simply 'being stubborn.' I tried to tell him about the coals having been doused, but that I still loved him, I just didn't have the fire for him anymore… Plus, at the moment, I was SICK!

It had only been a few weeks since it was actually an issue because of his medication kicking in. *Oh, God, how can I do this to him? Am I trying to pay him back for all those nights I wanted him, but was denied?* So, I tell him, "I'm sick, I'm exhausted… but, I'm open. So, just enjoy me, if you'd like to." *This did not feel anything like that one boy back in high school who made me feel used. This was giving of myself to someone I loved deeply. Maybe it could help heal some of his wounds from our marriage.*

To my surprise, instead of the gentleman he had always been, he rolled over and got on top of me without pause and started kissing me and feeling my breasts. I had nothing to put into it. I felt weird about that. But, I felt good that he was finally going to get some and enjoy it.

Afterwards, we had a really nice talk, which cleared the air about what just happened. It was such a loving, tender, sweet exchange and nothing, nothing, nothing about getting back together. He asked, "Is there more? You know, when you are with people the first time. Or is it still awkward at this stage of the game?"

I answered frankly, "When it is new, it's more awkward, it's more exciting, it's more tantalizing, it's more anticipation, it's more…everything. You know, you've just got to be able to get out there and explore your sexuality because there's a lot of catching up to do. And if you do meet someone, I hope that they'll be able to accept me as part of your life."

We agreed it was the best way to handle things. No harm done.

We continued to talk about things, like a brother and a sister. I told Lee how I had let go of dating this great guy–someone I was able to get past my jaded thoughts with and actually enjoy as a man. However, the piece of the relationship that was intimate had a similar pattern to that of Lee's and mine.

It was weird.

Lee seemed to feel better that he wasn't the only one I intimidated. I wasn't sure what the new man's issue was. I recognized my issue was to know when to stop trying to make it work. This wonderful friend gave me the perfect opportunity to practice this particular concern of my life. I am so appreciative of him in my life, *still*.

Lee was stunned, "So, stuff like that happens to other people? You mean I'm not the only one?" I said, "Honey, everything happens to other people." He was so relieved.

It was the middle of the night now, and I desperately needed to sleep but his snoring was so bad that I actually tape-recorded it. I laid there wide-awake, hoping that this was a springboard for him to be able to move on and start dating other women.

We are each very fortunate to have one another. We no longer have that constant sparring between us that we had when inside our marriage--not to say we never duke it out anymore, or snarl at one another... Nevertheless, I love him so dearly and he loves me like no one else does. Why let our decaying marriage ruin our love and friendship? The marriage was suffering, stagnating and hindering our growth as whole individuals. Our love and friendship were what kept us together.

Before we divorced, we coincidently met several people who lived their marriages 'outside of the box:' who stayed married but lived apart. Neither of us understood that very well, either. What is the point of marriage exactly? How do we really define it? That wasn't a solution for me.

Close friends and relatives, that wanted to see Lee and I get back together, frequently reminded me of our obvious love for one another. I was told I was kicking God in the face after being granted the wish I had prayed for so many years to manifest: Lee wanted to have sex with me. We decided to try to take advantage of his newfound sexuality and see if we could re-ignite the passion that had been there, the times that it was. I didn't want to make any decisions based on defiance or stubbornness. I felt I owed this a chance. But like a match struck, after the initial flare, the kindling was gone.

We finally agreed it was better to remain friends, without benefits. But, I had learned of companionship and what that means in life is much more important than just sex. The psychic we saw many years earlier was right. Our relationship was like that of huge pilings driven deep into the earth that even a hurricane couldn't destroy. What building, or structure, we put upon those pilings is for us to decide, or re-model as we see fit. We cleared the rubble, and started to build fresh from there.

I still think that sexuality is an essential part of a monogamous relationship, just by virtue of that relationship's very definition. By taking out that piece of the description that had caused us so much pain over the years and doing the long-avoided surgery, we have been able to continue in a *healthful companionship.*

So, that is the conclusion of the sexual part of the saga between Julie and Lee. We tried to be open to all potentialities, without counting on any particular outcome. Now, we just try to live in the moment, enjoy what we can with each other, and are happy being a supportive family to one another.

A friend, who is like a sister to me, gave me a beautiful poster by an artist named SARK. It was of a long rainbow with little clouds that had little sayings in them. The first one that caught my eye and kept presenting itself to me was one that I chose to live by:

Promise to marry yourself first and never leave. SARK

This planted a seed. At that time, I was working with ritual in my life. I was coming back to my Shamanistic studies, studying yoga fairly deeply, and really working at healing those wounds within me that had built up over the first four decades of my life (*and God knows how many lifetimes!*) I needed to parent myself. I needed to make the decisions for that child within me.

The concept of marrying myself meant to me that I was going to look after myself, financially, emotionally, sexually; *whether by myself or with someone.* It meant that I would care for myself and love myself the way I wished someone else would love me. That was an amazing, "*ah ha!*"

By consciously naming my intentions, the universe provided opportunity after opportunity, after opportunity for me to practice, cultivate and grow my *ability to care for myself.* Marrying myself became more and more a representation of my commitment to do so. I talked about it for a year. I knew it had to be special. I had to prepare for this righteous act on my soul's behalf.

I read an article in National Geographic on the twenty-five top places to visit in India. I had wanted to go there for a long time to study Yoga and Tibetan Medicine. *As long as I'm there I might do a little traveling, sightseeing.* As I paged through this dazzling guide, I saw a gorgeous picture of icicles dripping. Where in India are there icicles dripping? The article answered, *at the head of the Ganges Rivers.*

The legends say, to bathe in the Ganges River, one cleanses and purifies their sins. But to bathe at the *Headwaters* of the Ganges cleanses not only your own sins, but your family's for seven generations. *Well, a girl's gotta try when it's this easy. It's just a little pilgrimage... That was it!*

That was where I'd marry myself. I could do a pilgrimage before I started my studies. It was perfect! Tasha actually thought it was funny.

Others thought it was another, "Oh there goes quirky Julie again." When I told Lee about it, he kind of laughed, but he still was very kind and supportive. "That's my Boo. Only you would make a marriage ceremony for yourself."

We arrived at the Headwaters on the Summer Solstice, just as the sun was cresting over the glacier. A huge chunk of it, I don't know, maybe four stories tall, just cracked right off and splashed into the water--welcoming me! It was as if the glaciers were applauding the fact that I had made this most sincerely arduous journey up the mountain.

No matter how much I thought I had planned and prepared, I had no idea how it would test my strength and my capacity to persevere. I had planned to do the full Mikvah, dunking in Jewish tradition, but there was no place to actually go in all the way. This river, feeding this nation for thousands of years, poured upward and out from underneath the mountain, like a waterfall, but it was a 'watersurge' with such strength that I couldn't bathe the way I had expected to. That's okay. I did it the baptizing way, because that was what was available.

I found a little area behind a massive boulder where I could step in up to my ankles. The water, with chunks of ice floating by, was so cold that it burned my skin. I scooped and splashed several handfuls of water over my head, down my back, and over my body.

As I came out of that freezing water, some type of amazing colored hummingbird started to buzz around me. It wouldn't leave me throughout the rest of my ceremony. We were at about 13,400 feet. There was no vegetation in sight for miles. I couldn't figure out where in the world it had come from.

In some traditions, the hummingbird is a totem for learning to suckle the nectar of life, having the ability to quickly go from one place to the next, bringing nourishment, spreading the pollen, cultivating the nectar of life. It was so meaningful to me; I was even able to take pictures of it.

I stood atop the mountain (*really it was another 12,000 feet to the top but I was as atop as I was going to get of the Himalayan mountains.*) I realized that with all my preparations to get there, I didn't have a specific dialogue or prayer for my actual ceremony. My friend had given me a beautiful veil. I wrapped it around me. I felt like it was a *tallit* (the Jewish prayer shawl that one wraps oneself inside—to shut out the rest of the world—to be in one's own space with God.) Somehow or another, my body was doing what it thought it needed to do.

I said a prayer for myself, declaring my intentions and vows to care for myself, love myself, under all circumstances. The words flowed effortlessly, that's all I remember, but I do know that it felt just right. After, for a moment, while still inside the wedding veil, I contemplated what marriage to myself meant. I felt uncomfortable under the veil, and I thought, *"Why do women wear veils for their wedding?"* I burst out laughing. *"So we can't see what the hell we are getting ourselves into!"*

In recognizing this, my arms flung open and the wind caught the veil like wings coming off my body. I was ONE with everything for a moment. I was earth and sky, wind and water, and a burning flame all at once. I felt glorious. I felt love. I loved myself. I was my past, my present and my future. I felt myself as the universe.

At that moment, the quantum physics were jumping in my brain and I knew I had created the initiation for myself to move into the next level of knowledge, experience, and action. Thank God Jaxon (my cohort in India where it is extremely helpful to have a man traveling with you) made it to the top, too. He even caught my wings moment on film!

Being in India those two months, I had very amazing, wonderful moments and very humbling, wretched moments. There were times where I wished I could just go home. One of those days that I was really unhappy and ready to go home, I called Lee. He listened to me and let me vent and he said, "So how long would it take you to get back?" *Did he miss me? And want me to come home early, too?*

I figured in actuality, it would be about 4 days before I would hit New York--*I was almost in the 4th world.* He helped me gather my thoughts. "So, if you felt better in a few days and you came home, wouldn't you be pissed that you left this experience that you've been planning for over a year?"

I was surprised. That was a new level of maturity for Lee, because he knew that it was best for me to stay. Yes, he was becoming more Buddha-like each day, and he was right, I did feel better after a few days, and the rest of my experience truly was life changing. I had pride in myself that I had gotten to this place, understanding that life is all practice. I found inner strength that I knew I could muster on the behalf of others, but had not practiced on my own behalf. I was entirely on my own, across the world, and navigating through all the wonders and fears that I encountered. I can't forget that I did make some very good life-long friends there, but I will tell you that by the time I got off that airplane in Amsterdam a month later, I cried and cried. I wasn't even in the United States yet, but I was only one day away from home. I was in a place where I wasn't the oddity, I wasn't going to make some major social faux pas everyday, and there were people that would get my jokes. *Maybe.*

Lee - 8

I never doubted that we would be in each other's lives as best friends, ever. When we got married, I don't know if Julie was the right person to be my wife but today I am certain that she is the right person to be in my life. People did ask me, "How could you still want to have any kind of relationship with her after what she has done to you?" The answer must be the same reason as how could she want to have anything to do with me after what I have done to her. We went into this divorce that way. We were more friends in our marriage than anything else. That kind of friendship, a thoroughly loving friendship as we had, we continue to have.

However, the fact was, I'd never actually *lived* alone. This part was about me.

I went from living with my parents, to having roommates, to marrying Jules. The transition of living alone was extremely difficult, trying to figure out everything by myself, for myself, trying to schedule everything. You know; the grocery shopping, the cleaning help, and the plumber if there was a leaking toilet. It took a while, but I think that the transition has gone smoothly and I have managed very well. I have learned to schedule things based on when I can be there, or else I just make the time.

I do enjoy my peace, my quiet. There is still the great feeling of waking up and being alone in this house and just walking around in my pajamas, lounging and not having to answer to anybody. Not having to answer the phone if it rings, not having to have noise around me.

If I want to clean the dishes I do, which I generally do anyway. Sometimes, I will leave my coffee cup on the counter...on a Sunday...in the morning...for a couple hours. I know it sounds strange, but I can do that. That's my rebellion. I can sit on my couch with the fire going and just read a magazine. Don't get me wrong, I also miss having a family life here, as well.

When Tasha is here, running around, there is a lot of happiness. When she is not here, I can just get back into myself a little bit, which is nice, too. I do love being able to just get up and go at a moment's notice. It's something that really gives me thrills and chills.

I don't know how it got started, but Julie and I started having sex a while after my medication kicked in. We slept together a few times after we divorced, after Oscar passed away, it just happened.

It was fun. There were no intentions; there was nothing that I felt was going to start all over again, but it felt comfortable, it felt right. It was nice to have her in my arms intimately again. There was some awkwardness to it but it felt good. We had some great times with it. The first couple of times were wonderful. We were like bunnies--just having fun with it, starting fresh all over again, just enjoying it for what it was, and that was just raw pleasurable sex.

I remember walking into her house and she was in front of the sink and I grabbed her and kissed the side of her neck, squeezed her breast; she turned to liquid. I had stopped by for a little a.m. pleasure.

We were making love upstairs when we heard a knock at the door. Julie had called a plumber. She pointed him towards downstairs and we ran back upstairs to finish what we were doing. I was just so hot for her. We even talked about where our relationship was heading. I was not ready. It was turmoil for me.

Eventually your head starts taking over your body, you start thinking more like a couple. It becomes something discussed and talked about. What is the next step for a divorced couple (between us) that has gone through so much? Where are we going with this? What do we do now? Why are we doing this?

It doesn't need to go in that direction, it can be just for sex. It really can, but it didn't and I think it weighed more on Julie than it did on me that you know, that whole 'what should our next step be?' That question is one of those reasons why I didn't date for a long time. It tends to go in that direction. To find a woman that is okay with going out, having some sexual fun once in awhile, it's not very easy these days.

I didn't have any kind of preconceived notions for having sexual relations with her just to try to get her back. But, of course, that's eventually where it went to and eventually that's where it stopped. Our last intimate night together, Julie wanted to have sex to see if, *how did she put it,* if the candle could be lit and become this burning flame or fire, whatever.

It just didn't happen for her, and that hurt. But you know, we moved on from that. It was an experience; something we went through. We leave it at that.

All it did was make the mind work. Everything made me surer of myself; who I was and what I needed to do to be a better person. It made me realize that I wasn't where I thought I was and that I still have a long way to go to be honest with myself and what I want. It made me think before I say, versus say before I think. It made me realize just what is (and who are) family, and how important family is.

I don't hold anything against Julie. I still love her. Given the opportunity to have intimate times with her again, I'd probably jump on it, or her, ha ha! Why not? I'm human. In my opinion, we had some great, great sexual times. But, I wouldn't want it to go any further than that.

Another year passes and the two people that are most important in my life, in what I do and how I do it, were out of town for the whole summer. Julie was in India, and Tasha was at camp. So, I decided to just go ahead and buy something that I have wanted for so long, a Harley Davidson. It was very exciting for me. I was finally able to do something for myself the way that I wanted to do it. When, how, where I wanted to do it; everything! It was really, really cool.

It was the beginning of actually doing things that I've always wanted to do, but for some reason, had never done. I'm not the kind of person who is just going to sit on my ass all day and not do anything. I was now able to get out, by myself, nothing to hold me back. I had always dreamt of having a motorcycle. Now, I do.

Some people think it is a very lonely type of passion or hobby; it's not. You meet some interesting people when you stop. Groups form easily. But when you are riding alone on the bike, and there's only you and the machine and the road, there is a very peaceful existence in that.

With both Julie and Tasha gone, it did make me get out more, and do more things with other people. Even with all of the shit that Julie and I have gone through, I'm still happy to be with her a lot. But I have a few other friends in my life that I hang out with. They're a comfortable group.

My summer was very self-fulfilling. The Harley thing, to me, was as big of a deal in my life as Julie going to India was for her. For me, it was a huge step. No matter what, riding my bike is something I definitely enjoy doing during the spring, summer, and fall.

Tasha - 8

"Mommy can you hear me?"

"Oh my God, I hate Miss McDonald. I can't believe she assigned us pneumonia for our health report," said Suzy who was on the phone with her friend Chachi. "Yeah, I mean it's not like it's going to happen to anyone we know, right?" said Chachi.

"I know. What have you found out about pneumonia?" says Suzy. "Well, I have found out that it is water in your lungs and that it makes you want to drink tons of water, you?" said Chachi. "I have found out that it could put you in the hospital for a very long time," said Suzy. "Well we should get to bed so we will be ready for our presentation. See you tomorrow. Bye," said Chachi. "Bye," said Suzy.

It was early Monday morning and it was still dark, I was still sleepy. As I gazed through the school bus window, I heard sirens of an ambulance going off. I really didn't notice them until we pulled up to the bus stop across from my mom's house. I was staying at my Dad's this week, but they're just a few blocks away from each other, and on the same bus route.

There were a few police officers, firefighters, and EMT's scattered around. I thought it was for my neighbor's, who happen to be very old, so I didn't panic until Chachi came on the bus yelling for me to, "Get off the bus because something is wrong with your mom!"

I asked if she knew what was wrong with her. She said my mom couldn't breathe very well. I started to panic! Everything that my mom and I ever did started popping into my head. It was crazy. The one thing that kept popping into my head was when I was being born. I felt like an angel or something.

I rushed off the bus without grabbing my stuff and ran into my mom's house. Chachi's mom was there as well. When I saw my dad, I rushed over to him to give him a hug. My parents are divorced but they have a very good relationship. I started to cry but my dad told me everything would be all right. I looked over at my mom, but I couldn't see her because she was surrounded by paramedics. After they moved out of the way, I saw my mom with a big scary mask on her head. I was really scared to even go talk to her, but I did.

"Mommy, can you hear me?" I asked with fright.

She nodded her head up and down. I was relieved. My dad came and told me that, "Mommy had water in her lungs. It's bad. The paramedics called me right after you had left for the bus." He was sorry, but he had to rush over here right away. I hugged him very tight.

"Pneumonia," I said in a soft voice.

The EMT told us that Mommy had to be taken to the hospital right away so that they could help her. They said that we could bring her to the hospital. We talked for a while, and then we packed a bag for her and drove her to the hospital. Once we were there, they showed us to her room and took my mom to the doctor.

We made lots of signs for her room, and we put up some pictures of me and my dad. Once she got back to her hospital room, they gave us dinner and we stayed the night. The next day I had to go to school and my daddy had to go to work. We came back after school and work, and I told my mom about my day. She kept dozing on and off, but I didn't stop talking because I felt like she didn't want me to stop, even though she didn't say anything.

After a few days, Mom was all better. She still had to take medicine but that was all right. Everything was back to normal, and my mom and I became very much closer. Now I know that everything happens for a reason.

CHAPTER 8 DISCUSSION

Recognizing Beginnings

At this stage in history, the marriage institution is an entirely different thing than it was for the prior 5,000 years. Today, over half of the women are single, and over half of the marriages end in divorce. The scales have tipped, and we are, as a generation, searching for new definitions of love, family, and healthfulness in our lives. Lee and I recently read a beautiful obituary in the newspaper about a couple who had been married for 65 years. It said they were the quintessential 'marriage of the era.'

I think, for this era overflowing with divorces, there is no standard 'marriage of the era.' However, 'divorce of the era' may certainly be something historians reflect upon, as well as sociologists, economists, and let's not forget political principles. Why is it that Gays and Lesbians want the 'rights' that come with marriage? They can have any civil ceremony they want. Why is it more 'civilized' to have a 'legal' wedding.

Health insurance?

Prior to only 150 years ago, most women in the world had no choice about whom they married, how many children they had, who their income belonged to, or where they were allowed to venture without a man by their side. Even in the world today, we can witness injustices that are masked under the institution of marriage. In Africa, if a girl is not circumcised, she is not worthy of being a wife. Or here's a wretched one: if a man rapes her, he is obliged to marry her, as no one else will have her. *What existence is this, where women will douse themselves in fire to leave what is so fearful in everyday, every moment, of their life?*

I think millions of women already have done, and will continue to do so, (whatever they want to call it,) a dedication, or marriage, ceremony to themselves—where they anoint themselves to be the creative souls that they are supposed to be.

We can promise ourselves to never veil our self or our clarity again, or at least recognize those veils as they come. It's all practice. Life is all practice.

If you wake up unhappy with yourself, vow to yourself that you will immediately work to remedy that, because the relationship with yourself is the one that all other relationships are based on. If you are not true with yourself, you can't be true in your other relationships.

Say to yourself, if I do not witness my good and my bad and my beautiful and my ugly, I cannot have compassion for everyone else who has all those aspects in them as well. We don't want to believe we have ugliness in us but, in actuality, we each have all the seeds of everything in us. We are a universe unto ourselves.

Many traditional philosophies teach that the universe is made up of basic energies, usually: Water, Wind, Fire, Earth and Space (or some call this Metal.) These are but a few descriptions of the many types of energies that make up the 'life-force' energy, underlying all that is. Each tradition has their name for this life-force, this energy. In Chinese Medicine, it is called Qi (chi), whereas in Vedic philosophy, it is called Prana. These two words, meaning the same across the cultures, encompass ALL energies. Many traditions, including these two, include practices to learn to control the energies in our bodies and around our beings. Utilizing the breath is one of the first teachings (although there are sects where breathing practices are held off for months, possibly years, in order to train the body and mind to prepare for the practice of these powerful techniques.)

Breathing is the very essence of our life-force. We have only minutes to survive without breathing, unlike food or even water. The breath is what determines a life is born alive, and when a life ends. In between, it nourishes and cleanses every single cell of our bodies in a miraculous alchemical process of exchanging the gases of O_2 and CO_2.

Learning about our breathing patterns helps us to recognize our habits related to our optimal health, meaning on all levels of existence: physical, mental, emotional and spiritual. By witnessing these small habits, we learn to feel what the emotion is that is attached to the habit. We use the mental practice to analyze the physical practice of our breath when we are emotionally experiencing, say, perhaps fright: do we hold our breath; perhaps breathe very shallow and quick; or do we pucker our lips and blow, or sigh. Moreover, how does the stomach feel, or the fingers or toes… where does fear present itself in your body? Or love, anger, joy, courage or any other emotion. And what do those emotions do to the breath?

Where do any of these emotions show up in the body, how do they feel, and what might be the spiritual aspect for our total entity with that emotion? Is it something overgrown which needs weeding, or is it something which needs some tending to proliferate? For example, I had witnessed that I could cry instantly, but laughing was something stifled, for whatever reasons. I wanted to cultivate more laughter in my life. There are actually laughing 'classes' taught by Yogis around the world. I'm happy to watch a funny movie, but there is nothing like a laugh that makes you cry, and afterwards…

I offer you, next time that happens to you, to notice your breathing… what's the energy in your body like after you're all laughed and cried out? First you have to catch your breath. Next, one usually lets out some extra big sighs. Then there is a calmness (unless a little tickle of a laugh comes back, especially when you're at a funeral or some major meeting and no one really gets your joke but you…) that pervades your body. It is as if there is a glow about the body, just like the one after a passionate session of making love, or a yummy nap.

Another thing I noticed about my energies and habits was that when I really needed to cry, when it was painful to hold it back but I refrained anyways, at one point I could not deny that I would find myself with a sore throat and respiratory ailment by the next day. The energy of the needed cry was blocked in my throat, right where it would hurt when I would hold the cry inside and not let it out. Now, I make sure I get it out of me, even if I have to wait, I know that holding it in will only make me sick. Literally.

I believe if we breathe consciously once a day for ten breaths, we will not only see an improvement in our health and mental faculties, but we will find emotions that we have buried, waiting to be freed on the wave of the breath, to leave the body and be alchemically transformed into nourishment. Decay can destroy us or nourish us, smother us or give us room to grow. Using the breath as a visualization of releasing that which is not healthful on the exhale, and bringing in health with each cleansing breath will not only calm our minds, but rejuvenate our bodies, cell by cell. The more we exhale, the more room we have to bring in fresh nourishing breath.

As we learn to watch the breath, we simultaneously learn to control it. We can do this by simply breathing those intentions into our being and exhaling that which would keep us from attaining our goals.

Next time you find exhilaration on your path, (whether on a Harley, or atop a mountain, or watering the garden,) witness it. How does it feel? Where do you feel it? What happens afterwards? Then, imprint that in your mind and body, so that you may call upon it next time you need a lift. ☺

Evocations:

1. Can I, under the most duress, recognize my 'purpose' for being?
2. How will I persevere or make it through difficulties?
3. What can I do that I have pride in and enjoy?
4. Can I be the spouse to myself that I desire for myself? What does it mean to be our own spouse?
5. Can I give to myself what I feel I am lacking from outside of myself--as a spouse? Parent? Confident? Mentor? Advisor? Child? Friend...?
6. Where do I 'feel' what is right or wrong?
7. What does the topography of the "Emotional Map" of my body look like?
   Draw it! ☺

CHAPTER NINE

Smooth Sailing

Julie

I finally realized that my aspiration when I grow up is to be a wanderer, a mystic and a healer. I want to combine the three of them by learning the various traditions around the world. I'm not talking about wandering because I am lost, but wandering with purpose: to actually seek, and reach out to, all the opportunities that lie ahead; to learn and utilize a blending of the common historical threads; and, to share that gathered wisdom with other wanderers and seekers whose paths I cross.

One of the things I've learned through my studying of Yoga, Taoism, Buddhism, Christianity, and Judaism is that they all have that same message of karma. *What you plant, you shall reap.* Having dealt so deeply in all these different studies, it was now time to use them as nutrition for my new growth. I felt I was ready, but needed to remember, some structures must come down before we can rebuild...

When I did come home from India, there was much, much to deal with. My mother was dying. Her home had flooded recently and nobody had even noticed. My home had flooded, too. It took me a week to get the two of them cleaned up and then, torrential rains came again, and both houses flooded a second time. I was overwhelmed with trying to take care of two homes, finishing papers for the University, starting a new business, and being a mother to my now-teen-aged daughter who had also just returned home from camp... Our family needed some re-connecting time.

I was stretched, like most of my peers and friends, and this generation of SUPER WOMEN!!! We do it all and are the best at getting done what needs to be done. We are more productive when we are busy. We care for our families and homes, parents and sick relatives or friends, managing the lives of many people, and then, on top of it, we work... and volunteer, walk the dog (not as much as the dog would like, I'm sure of that) and try to maintain some semblance of a social life. Maybe we're also taking classes through all this, in something new and interesting that catches our attention. And with our independence, so too, comes the responsibility of being the role models for the future generations of women. We had no role models to show us how to "do it all" as the happy homemaker and the CEO.

Our heritage must come from those women who gave birth in the fields and then kept working while the newborn suckled...

When it comes to life's challenges, (as resilient as I may seem to others) people are sometimes very amazed to find out how much fear I have. They think that I live and make my decisions without fear and so boldly, *without caution*, I often hear. I have chosen, in my self-study, to use my fears to help me evolve. The first step with any one of them, for me, is always the hardest--it is recognizing and naming that fear.

I believe there are two emotions, and everything else is based off those:

Love and Fear...

Fear of not being loved or lovable, or even loving: or fear of having no love: an absence of it. I've debated this with people for several years now.

I think a piece of maturing, growing and having an understanding about love, is learning there are so many levels of love. There are so many people to love. They don't all equate to the same kind. I think one of the most common things I can make an analogy to, is how often I've heard women who are pregnant with their second child, who question "How will I ever love a second child as much as I love the first?" Nevertheless, they find out they are perfectly capable of loving the second, third and all to come, in their own way, for who each child is and will be in the world.

If we all truly based our decisions on Love, which had a definition deeper than that of the drug of 'In Love' defines. We think we have a definition of what love is, but love is so much more--like the Eskimos have 140 or some terms for snow. We have this one word '*love*' that we think encompasses all that it is. Yet, there are so many levels, hues, manifestations, and shapes of Love--that happen in, and of, love--that to create from them with passion is encompassing all that *love* is.

From this deeper understanding of the many definitions of Love, we can move from a balanced center, rather than be thrown off course due to circumstances. We can stay firmly planted and yet, not be torn asunder from external conditions that might normally instill *Fear* in us.

Fear has a couple acronyms I like to quote:
1. **F**uck **E**verything **A**nd **R**un
2. **F**alse **E**xpectations **A**ppearing **R**eal

The Rabbi at Tasha's Bat Mitzvah had spoke about us being truly able to find God when we find the ambiguity in everything as the beauty of God. It is said that there are 49 ways to take any particular thing or experience and create positivity out of it. There are also 49 ways to create negativity out of it. This is very interesting to me and is fairly close to the Tibetan Book of the Dead, where when one dies, the deceased must face their 49 angels and 51 demons. The Tibetans say there are more ways to create evil than there are to create goodness. In order to evolve, whether they instill fear or not, the question is—do we face our demons? So, fear is, to me, something that I need to look at and wonder *why I am fearful*. What is frightening about this situation? So, when I face my worries, it's not blindly. Rather, it is a conscious decision where I am quite aware of all of the ramifications of which I can conceive. Yet, I must simultaneously realize that there are those consequences of which I can't even imagine, whether they are based in fear or love.

One thing we all just have to accept at some point is that FEAR will hit us smack in the face at exactly the moment we need it. In order to witness and name our fears, we must consciously intend to do so. *But, watch out! Moreover, remember to qualify how you call those fears to come to you. Ask for gentleness!*

However, at this point in my evolution, I choose to use my life experiences, use my fears, and use my urges. When I say urges, I mean when I am urged to help someone, or when I am urged to write or sing or dance, eat, make love or sleep, that I listen to those urgings. I've learned to pay attention and to realize, or actualize, them. I have chosen consciously to use each one of my gray hairs that I have accumulated as the foundation and fertilizer of the garden of my-self.

I think that the message we are giving to our daughter to cultivate into her own life is:

"How can you learn to live with the knowledge that all things will change? And, how can love, as an energy, can be given and received on various levels?"

I can't say enough how good it feels that Tasha loves me and trusts me, and that she knows I love her and am here for her. It doesn't matter that her father and I have different languages of *love* for her. *She can speak several languages!*

I did try to give Lee what he needed from our marriage. I just wasn't very good at it. He did try to give me what I needed. He wasn't very good at it, either. What a paradox we both are. I did really well as a wife, for several years; I used to make dinner every night, the house was always immaculate…I was the quintessential 'good wife,' but it was hard for me to maintain and certainly didn't leave room for my free spirit to roam and wander, nor fulfill what I expected of companionship. I don't know if being a 'good wife' is a gene that I didn't get, because I just wasn't able to be that woman and still be me, this woman that I am, today.

It may sound a little whiney, but I need a wife or two of my own.

This whole idea of dating, what does it mean? Does it mean that you're trying to find someone to marry? Is that the goal of dating? Who has time to find anyone, now that time is running almost twice as fast as it did 50 years ago and our lives are so full since all the *technology to make our lives easier* just gives us more to do?

I know there are MANY divorced people out there wondering why to even bother getting married again. It's not about giving up on love; it's about the institution of marriage—what it has meant historically, versus now.

If you like to know where language comes from, you might want to look up the history of the words 'husband' and 'wife.' Usually, husbandry is associated with impregnating animals. A waif was a servant who was not allowed to buy their freedom, yet a step above a slave. Generally, though, a waif went with the other belongings of a property, usually to the surviving brother. Don't get me started, my editor won't let me pontificate here... (but blog me!)

In dating, job interviews, or really, any other relationships, either we present ourselves as who we truly are even though we might be afraid that person won't love (hire...) us for who we really, truly are. Otherwise, we might end up trying to become someone different, which we think is what they want. We give away little pieces of ourselves and we hide little things that we wouldn't want them to know because they might not like us if they knew those secrets, or skeletons. So if I'm going to put time into a date, or a hire, rather than living in fear of them finding out those things—months or years down the road—I figure, let's just put it all out there right now. If it's not going to work in the long run, let's just recognize that now and not waste either of our time.

I've come to a place in my life where it is more important that people hold me in their esteem, not because I conform, but because I am honest, even when not conforming. There are those that have issues with my not conforming, and have held hostage, or let's say negotiated their affection or attention or acknowledgement, because of my damned refusal to conform to their values or judgments.

I'm not judgment free by any means. I, then of course, have to look at whom I have decided not to have in my life just because they don't conform to what I need in my parameters of the people to whom I give my affection, attention and acknowledgment.

I have learned to recognize that when I am indignant about something, and then I gather the nerve to say something and it's brushed off, or ignored or de-valued, when that happens, I realize the issue is not going to be resolved or closed. How do you make someone be open to a closure of something that they claim does not exist or is worthy of attention? How can they possibly put closure on something they do not see or comprehend?

Lee and I have had very strong disagreements about when it's ok to lie and when it's not. The problem with lying is that one deceit begets another, begets another, begets another… pretty soon, you have to ask other people to lie for you in order to keep the fabrications going. Lee already knew this, just from our marriage. We'd always have to discuss what I was 'allowed' to know, or talk about with his family, and what I was not, when we went to family gatherings.

Lee recently called and asked, "Are you mad at me about this latest thing with Tasha today?" I replied, "I'm not mad at you. I think Tasha played us both, and I'm not mad at her either, because why shouldn't she play by what rules she knows?"

From my perspective of the story, Tasha had gotten in some trouble at school. Lee agreed we should ground her and asked if I thought it should be for this weekend or the following weekend. My response was that consequences should always be as close to the deed as possible. Because she was honest with us about it before we found out about it from the school, her consequence should be less. So one weekend, and it would be this weekend. Anyhow, next weekend was the SnowDaze Dance at her school. So, to teach her that we as parents do not condone this kind of behavior, we grounded her for the current weekend. I found out later through Tasha that Lee told her I wanted to ground her for the weekend of the dance, too, and that he talked me out of it!! I couldn't help myself.

"WHAT?!"

He was totally caught, and Tasha knew it. I love the guy, but I really don't have to protect him like that anymore. She gets very mixed messages between us sometimes and I feel we all need to be accountable for what we say and do. I immediately told Tasha my account of the conversation, and confronted Lee about it in front of her. Honesty is worse when you have to face it the second round, for sure. But, I can't ground him, now, can I? *He's a big boy and can own his actions and words.*

In poor Oscar's case, it got to the point where the lies were so accumulated; he simply couldn't unbury himself from them. They cracked down and crushed his entire world that was only built on the perceptions of his lies.

Our Western society is so entrenched in a chemical basis but really, the universe is based on physics, on energetic patterns and the fact that energy only changes. It isn't made and it isn't destroyed, it just changes patterns.

So from a scientific point of view, we are all energetic beings infused with chemicals and their reactions. But from a religious point of view, we do all return to dust. And then, from a spiritual point of view, we are all of one and the same. We are just different energetic patterns of it and our energy affects the energy around us much like a tuning fork when struck will resonate and create other pitch forks to start vibrating as well. Even when the first one has had a hand or something placed on it to have it stop vibrating, the others will continue with their own vibration. The ones that are of the same key will vibrate stronger and longer than the ones that are in a different key, or pitch. But the fact of the matter is, even hearing different pitches; you can still affect one another, blend with one another, or even cancel the other out.

This is a concept I want to explore further than in this book, but… just to pose the wonder out there… If we can cancel the noise of our car engines with a device that is set at the same calibration, but on opposing intervals, like headphones cancel unwanted sound by generating an antisound (antinoise) of equal amplitude and opposite phase. The original, unwanted sound and the antinoise acoustically combine, resulting in the cancellation of both sounds.

DO PEOPLE'S ENERGETIC 'Vibes' DO THE SAME?

Furthermore, there is the whole magnetic concept where opposites attract or repel. This is the basis of my reason for being, to study these phenomena through relationships and their evolutionary shifts. I feel that each of us, as a soul, has our own signature imprint, manifested in physicality, and that in each and every one of us (or in the plants, the animals, or the earth,) are all these energetic patterns. Some people like to call it the 'grid.' The way I look at it, in being this energetic manifestation, my philosophy is that we're here to embody vibration, to learn how to create resonation at a higher frequency and pitch.

In doing this self-study, it all comes back to finding purpose in life through some of the hardest times of life. Most days that I recognize this, I am able to delight in it. It does help me face the adversity and the challenges in my life with a bit more joy. I started to create a basis of positive change with the concept of "Relational Shifts." The idea is that change is the only natural cycle in life. How we accept change and deal with it are what affect the world and manifest the butterfly effect. Because one person can change the world and have influence over another that might have influence over many others, and so on…

We're creating this book to support a positive change in the world regarding a subject that has mostly been looked upon as the reason for the decline of society. It **is** the decline of society, as we've known it; the world is coming to an end as we have known it. Today, there are more women than ever before in written "history" that are single or postponing marriage and children. So much has changed in only one or two generations. With the world shrinking the way it is through media and technology, girls and women are becoming validated citizens of the world. It is creating a change that no one really planned for.

I definitely feel that my journey has been (like many women in my age group that affect the world around them,) about learning to rely on myself, yet learning to ask for help when I need it is just as important. To expect the kind of love/fulfillment that I've searched for outwards in life can only come from within me and for me. In that sense, I can become swept up in the current of my life, and seem selfish.

I have realized that I do need to rely on others at certain times, which is a big barrier to overcome for me. I've had some wonderful people to rely on, and I've had some people that veritably seem to sabotage me. Knowing who to trust has been a big obstacle for me to overcome. I have learned how important it is to know whom it is you are talking to and how it is they need to hear what you want them to hear--through **their** language. When you can do this (and I have not quite mastered it-by any means,) you get them interested in what you want them to be interested.

Part of what has gotten better since we've divorced is that we do listen to each other much more now. With Lee and I, even when we had attempted to re-unite after Oscar died, the only way our relationship survived was that our communication skills were better, both listening and speaking our truths. Lee was really beginning to say how he felt, at least when he was honest with himself about it.

What happened was I had the realization that the connection wasn't working that way between us, the frequency was still discordant or something to that effect. I was trying to have integrity to myself. I realized there was just no way that I could go back to what we had, and that the only way to go forward was to release trying to recapture what we had. Thankfully, eventually, Lee came to understand that I wasn't trying to hurt him or get back at him, but, that I was trying to say the truth as lovingly as I could, even though it was painful. *I still practice daily.*

Some told me that ending my marriage would teach my daughter to give up rather than to persevere through the difficulties in relationships. A number of other people kept telling us to share our story, encouraging us to write a book about how our family used our divorce to create a better family than what we had before. I felt it was more important to teach her to reach for her dreams than to give pieces of her self away, change herself or, for that matter, try to change others in order to afford a principle that was other than ideal. We feel she has learned, through her own hardships with family and friends, that she can be aware of others' and be good to them, do service for them without expectation of return, but she does not need to put others' needs above her own. She can be "kind" while maintaining her uniqueness and direction. She does not have to comply to be accepted.

We have done what we can to teach Tasha about integrity, through what she might want to emulate, as well as through what she knows she will never do in her life, or with her children. Now, her life is an open road where she will explore the *in's and out's* of it, with me and her dad behind her to pick her up if she falls. However, we also give her the time to pick herself up, dust off and keep going. That is teaching her to care for herself, which is what we think our job really is about, teaching her to care of herself, as well as others or the earth.

We all recognize that this story is not only our own. It doesn't matter who has the affair, or what was the actual "goat-prod" that pokes us forward when we are getting lazy on our journey in life.

By the way, one of those women who prodded me ever so painfully years ago, by laughing at my real estate career and PTO commitments…She said, "Wow, Julie, of all people we went to high school with, I thought for sure you'd be doing something way bigger and better with your life."

WOW-ch! But, here I am, ten years later, absolutely feeling that I am doing everything I am meant to do. I am a mother, a storyteller, a healer, a shaman, an executive, an actress, producer, writer, scientist and many labels more.

Thank you, Karen! Now, there's proof of the power of our own little ripples causing waves

Some, not so encouraging, ask me, "Who do you think you are? What do you think you're doing? What makes you think anyone cares what you have to say? What makes you think you can succeed where others better than you have not?" And we ask ourselves, why? At this stage, I think those questions in our lives make us question ourselves and that is a positive thing, as long as we don't let those questions make us give up. We need to allow for 'goat-prods' to keep us going, right? That is a major hurdle for anyone to overcome when they have to make a decision for themselves, which goes against the status quo.

The answer is that as we have shared tidbits of our story with others, we, of course, hear of others' stories, too. Many have shared things with us after hearing what we've been through, that they would not even tell their therapist or best friends. That is the point of this book: to open dialogue, to flash a light on those dark spaces within us and clean out our cobwebs and skeletons. When we come clean, there is nothing hanging in the back of our mind needing protection.

When sharing life experiences of "Relational Shifts," it's as if we're having hot chocolate (as opposed to chicken soup!) Hot chocolate is nourishing, stimulating and is even filled with anti-oxidants to wash away the toxins we accumulate in life. How this all fits in is that with the studies I have done over the years, all that has been taught to me, are the things that Lee and I utilized in our divorce. There have been philosophies, thought processes, and practices that we have used to help heal our family. Now, we each feel mutually loved, accepted and supported and encouraged in ways we hadn't necessarily felt when we were married.

My research in learning these techniques and processes encouraged us to put it into the general public's hands through creative work. If we are able to help any other families through our personal story, than that is our blessing. Our platform has some educational aspects that hopefully won't even be noticed, but their seeds will be planted. It is your garden to do with as you please.

I had come home; I had lived the third act. I had married myself and now was ready to put it to work. To take the manure, the muck of the things that have happened in my life and to use it wisely to create a garden; to cultivate something that would not only be beautiful for my family and myself, but for anyone who could allow themselves to partake of that garden. The process of writing this book over the last few years has been like going through psychoanalysis on a daily basis, but with no certified therapist along the way…Oh, but I do truly have many therapists in my life whom I can call without an appointment, and blather away for an hour for the small price to being the same for them. SOCIAL THERAPY, I like to call it. PEER-TO-PEER advice…

I haven't been around for my friends much while I've been working on the book (and her sisters, the website and the episodic series.) It's like I've been giving birth to triplets all year, one at a time. I've been telling my friends and family that I will soon re-surface from this 'labor' I've been in, but, like Tasha's birth, it's taking wayyyy longer than I thought it would. With Tasha, I thought I would have a home birth, maybe in the bathtub, with candles and music playing, and this incredibly joyous event. I had it all planned out. Instead, it took 30 hours of labor and I ended up with every medical instrument attached, inserted or hooked up to me that they could use. I had a C-section, and the doctors helped bring Tasha to her destination of this life. As a student and a teacher, she arrived.

I didn't really know what to do with this new role in my life, but I knew I'd do my best. Even when I fail her, and I have many times, her presence in my life inspires me to guide her by my own 'being.' I beam with pride when I see her look a waitress in the eye and greet them, or when I play piano and she comes to my side, as I did with my own mother those times she and I connected—singing together. Those little things that make me cry from their sweetness BALANCE those times she gives me 'the look'—the one she learned from me... Yet, she is of Lee in all his good and bad, and still, again, she is of her own future self that called its life into being through us.

At her Bat Mitzvah, I gave her 'the key' to her own garden. When a child goes through the Jewish initiation into adulthood, especially of their own volition, they take the responsibility of their life into their own hands. At that point, the child's successes and failures become their own.

This book's birth contrasts what now seems an easy birth with Tasha. I have been in 'labor' for weeks. I feel this book-child has also called its life forward through us, as a family. This book is long awaited by many souls attending this school of life.

I was now ready to grow with this book, and God bless Lee. He is at a place in life where he wants to support what I do, yet still take care of himself. He has felt guilty that he didn't do that in earlier years. Now, he is my familial support and ally in life. He knows I am that for him, as well.

My *(95-yr-old auntie)* Tanta and I were talking the other day. I told her of my dreams for when I grow up, to be a wanderer and mystic and healer. She laughed aloud. I asked what she thought was so funny, didn't she know me well enough to expect something like that?

She lovingly replied, "No, honey, what's funny is that I don't know when you are going to grow up!"

Lee - 9

With the way the world is today, the way life is going so fast, with technology proving what we can do, and how much we can do in a given day; it is very difficult. I can't imagine myself married right now, with the stupid phone that I have....every time it rings, I run to it.

I can't see myself getting into a committed relationship at this point. I mean, I'm not a selfish person, but I'm being selfish in the sense that I don't want anybody encroaching on my life right now. I want to be able to do what I want, when I want and not have the responsibility for anyone other than Tasha, or myself. I do feel responsibility for Julie, too. I want to make sure that she is okay.

My family, my dad, those are other kinds of responsibilities I want to be able to deal with. But, to deal with an outside person that I might not have feelings for, I just don't want to go there right now, at all, period. I don't mind going out on dates, and I've been on plenty. There were some girls I liked but just don't want to take it any further than where it's gone. It's just part of the transition, I suppose.

During our marriage, I was a very insecure person. I probably didn't like myself very much with all the outside stuff happening, like my parents, the business, marital problems... My way of taking the pressure off me was to tell Julie, "That it was all in your head".

Julie and I used to wrestle and she would say that it took away her sexual tensions. But did it really take away her sexual *needs*? It was something we put onto ourselves, into our own heads, that somehow didn't make us feel so bad about it.

I had a fear of change. I didn't flee. I couldn't fight. I was paralyzed by it. It's as if you put yourself against a wall where you feel that you are alone and vulnerable. The only one that can help you at that point is yourself. That's life, baby.

For me, processing our divorce, my tumor, and the intricacies of our families' relationships were very difficult. It would put me in a depressive state. You can get the counseling, you can talk to friends, but you're still the one who has decided to stay in, or leave, a hole called **Victimhood**. It's a good place to go experience and walk in circles for awhile; you're always going to get back to where you started. When you do climb out, that is when you realize you need to find a different path; you're rejuvenated, even if a little beaten up.

I had a great teacher. I had a great companion to help me, who guided me through. Julie didn't brainwash me, but she did wash my brain.

"I like myself." I can say that. I can talk to myself. It's okay. There is nothing wrong with that. Knowing that makes a big difference. Yeah, it's just security. There was no major turning point. It definitely didn't happen over night, it's a gradual progression. It takes effort, a conscious realization. It was worth going through the pain, going through all of it. It makes you stronger; it makes you like yourself more.

Today there is no way that I would try to do it any differently. I can't imagine what I would have missed. I cannot. I don't want to even think about that. It would have been more painful not to have worked on having a relationship with my family. Julie always said that it is easier to point out than to point in. It's just not worth it to stay bitter and angry.

I personally like the way we are. There is definitely a change. I'm sure a lot of that has to do with this hetero relationship that we have. The way we do things is so abnormally normal for real, whether at family functions, just the two of us going to dinner, or trips that we have taken as a family. I enjoy Julie's company very much. I enjoy her conversation. I enjoy everything about her.

I've even changed the way I feel about her with other men. I used to have major, major issues with Julie dating or having a boyfriend. I can't fake that kind of being happy for someone, when I am not happy. This genuineness, that's being happy for a friend—when they are happy and I see their joy.

People have a hard time looking at us without thinking that there are ulterior motives of our feelings towards one another, instead of taking our feelings as they truly are. People in my life are always saying, "You guys get along so well, why don't you get re-married?"

What is the idea behind marriage that supposedly makes everything good? When you and I both know that a lot of problems start right after you get married. It's so true. Any person Julie has dated or that I have dated will have a hard time with our relationship. They can't look outside the box. Some can't trust their own feelings towards Julie without being jealous no matter how cordial I am, especially if he's insecure about himself. But

I can understand that because I know that I was jealous in the beginning, too. You just have to move forward, know that there are different levels of love that you can have.

Under the circumstances of where we were going after we divorced, we most definitely had to work a lot harder to maintain our family.

I think as divorced parents, we make more of an effort to communicate versus just taking it for granted. Trying to maintain a friendship is almost as hard if not harder than maintaining a marriage.

I think we've grown up as individuals, which makes us better people, thereby enabling us to be a better family.

Marriage is contractual. When you are married, you have to make agreements. Not even agree, but somehow compromise as a married couple even though it's not exactly what you believe. I can't change Julie from what she wants to do or her beliefs whether I agree with them or not. Nor does she have to compromise with me. We can do whatever we like. She might try to put some of these beliefs on me and I'm definitely willing to listen, but you won't see any kind of organic milk in my house.

We were living under the same roof for a week (on a family vacation that we take each year in Palm Springs,) and I compromised by picking up the organic milk just to make it easy. It's not that big of a deal. *At my house, my daughter can have regular milk.*

Julie and I communicate about Tasha on a daily basis. Whether she is here or there, I feel I know what is going on her life, what she is doing, where she is going and who she is with. *But at times, I feel entirely disconnected, too.* Sometimes our schedules are all so different and so much can happen in just a few days, so if I'm out of town, or their schedules are too busy, I can feel left out. Julie feels the same way, too, I know. She still gets jealous, I think.

Julie, Tasha and I live an extremely *abnormally normal* family life, other than not living under one roof. We try to have weekly family nights when we go out together. Usually, we'll let Tasha decide on the restaurant, if we go out for dinner, and that generally means it's *Crossroads Deli.* She's like me that way, loves to go back to her favorite places. Julie and I also go out together, without Tasha, just to talk about life, school, raising our child, holidays, and trips. As a family unit, I think we're still pretty much intact. When it comes to what 'the normal family' does in this world, I can't think of any instance where we're not normal, other than the marriage piece.

I think when you look at Tasha today, and you see how well adjusted she is, it makes a dad proud. I can't think of anything that we should have done differently with her. She has become this bright girl that loves us both incredibly and loves the differences in each of our personalities. She is very good with her friends in talking to them about issues the way we talk to her. We've taught her to live with integrity, to be truthful, as hard as it may be.

She not only loves her friends, but has feelings toward all different types of people. She is definitely a very independent girl. She's not reserved. She's very open, like her mom. Sure, Julie and I have had big disagreements about Tasha's school or shopping, but that's okay. As a divorced couple, you don't even have to agree to disagree, even though we do.

Tasha likes to shop. She likes to buy clothes. It's not something Julie likes or does for enjoyment, but she goes because she has to. I do enjoy it and don't mind taking Tasha. She has gotten a lot better about valuing what she is buying, not purchasing just to purchase. As she grows and matures she's become more responsible in terms of how she is spending and what she is buying. It's also the same way with her studying. She is doing well in school. She is so mature because she learns from watching the interaction and struggles between Julie and me.

I think one main thing that Tasha has learned from me is that you can change if you want to. You can change your personality, change the person you are to the person you want to be. She has said to me on numerous occasions how when I used to yell, it would make her stomach turn, but now I talk to her more. She has seen me change as a man, that I am self-sufficient and that I live a good life, a happy life as an individual. *She might not have thought I could do that while Julie and I were getting a divorce.*

As in most any relationship, a marriage takes time and commitment. When you get divorced, you still are related to that person, but it's shifted. You still have relatives through this person, and friends, community... You can commit yourself to a job or to raising kids, but if you don't put into it what it needs, it's not going to settle down and wait. You're going to get fired from your job; your kids are going to become delinquent. I've learned you have to put into your marriage as much as anything else. I did not, and that was my mistake.

Now, our relationship has never been better. We still fight, we still get into arguments, but we have a lot of love and a lot of respect for each other as people. I've loved watching Julie grow and I'm sure she enjoys watching me succeed.

My latest success came to my attention through a very dear friend of mine. He wants to write something for me, about me. See, I've been talking to him throughout his divorce proceedings, giving him positive potentials and helping him see his own piece of the de-struction of his marriage. He is almost through with all of it, but they have never even brought in a lawyer. He is filled with joy that his in-laws of 30 years still love him and consider him family. He's been able to divorce without it having to be hateful.

This is the first 'family' I know I've helped through sharing my story. It may not have saved their marriage, but it did save their family. I feel pretty good.

We had a small party for the launch of Julie's company last year. I bought her a framed picture I knew she would like (even though I didn't like it.) I've changed. I know better now what she likes. I knew that it wasn't something that I wanted her to like. I wasn't looking to impress her with it. I was just giving her something I knew she would appreciate this time. *Because it wouldn't go in my house!*

My dad called me the other day. He said, "You know, Lee, I've never told you this but... I am so proud of you, so proud of you and Julie."

It's the first time he has ever said this so I asked him, "What for?"

He said, "You know, the way you guys are, the way you have kept your family together...it's very...well, I'm proud of both of you. In fact, I'm proud of all three of you."

I asked him what made him say that now. He said he has many friends down in Florida who talk about their kids being divorced and the lawyers and business's being closed and families being ripped apart. He gets to tell them about us and how we did it.

He is saying all this with such pride that tears well in my eyes. Of all the things in my life I have done to try to please him or make him proud of me, my divorce makes him the proudest. It is somewhat strange in a paradoxical way. Nevertheless, it was still very nice to hear it from him. *I'm not afraid, anymore, to being open about what happened in our marriage.*

The healing process is something that you have to continue doing. It goes on and on and on. I've got a lot of great memories that Julie and I have made over seventeen years, whether they are funny ones, sad ones, or tragic ones. We have had a good life together.

One last story...I went to bed the other night and was almost asleep. Tasha walked in my room around midnight to let me know she was 'bored.' I asked her what she wanted at this time of night, and she said she was going to go cook. I said, "Have fun, and clean up after." I rolled over to go back to sleep, but instead laid awake for a few moments after she walked out, and thought, "*What the hell am I doing? She wants to be with me and I'm going to choose sleep over that?*"

I followed the scent of butter into the kitchen to find her making pancakes. It was so sweet. We were on the opposite sides of the counter than we usually are, this time I was sitting and she was standing over the stove cooking for me. I asked her where she learned to make the best pancakes I've ever tasted. She said, "By watching Mom. I picked it up."

We don't even comprehend all that we have given her, and then she goes and improves it! Bravo! *That's my girl!*

Tasha - 9

Mommy,

Hey, how are you? I'm good. I miss you! Hmm, I need fancy clothes! Ha ha. We should like go to H & M, I LOVE it there! Hey, okay, camp is great, so much fun and other than having six girls in my cabin, we have fifteen, that's crazy! LOL, kinda weird but it's okay! LOL. How's the work stuff going? But yeah, second session I'm getting really excited for! I Love you so much. I have to go, we are walking to the park. Ha ha ha. Hope all is well but yeah, tell me if you see pics of me on the camp webpage, LOL. I LOVE you so much! Love you, write back.

Love you, bye.

Love always, Tasha

Happy B-day

I can talk to my mom about girl stuff. My dad and I always joke around about what boys I like or stuff about my friends, more about the gossip that goes on at my school because I know that he won't take it as seriously as my mom might. I think all my friends really like my mom and dad. They love how they are not married and still best friends.

Sometimes, I tell one of my parents something and they'll tell the other one. And then, I'll just be like, ah, kind of either embarrassed or shocked that the other person told that person. But when I ask one of them, "Oh, don't tell Dad or don't tell Mom," they tend not to.

My mom totally embarrassed me recently. She told one of my friends that when I was younger I used to take the poop out of my diapers and put it all over the walls. I wasn't even there to defend myself or stop her! My dad totally embarrasses me when we are somewhere where I don't want to be seen. On purpose, he'll like blast some music or something in his car.

At the time of my Bat Mitzvah, my dad and I would watch the show, *My Sweet Sixteen*, on TV. A joke we played on Mom would be like, "Oh, right, right, and when the Bat Mitzvah is done, we can start planning the sweet sixteen because that's the big one."

She would get very annoyed. Really, I know that for my sweet sixteen, I'll probably have a little party. I know that it definitely takes a lot of money and I don't want to do that to my parents because I know that they are exhausted from this last bash. Ha-ha.

With all the money that I received for my Bat Mitzvah, I kept half of it for myself and my banking account, and the other half was for me to go shopping for girls my age who are less fortunate than me. I had gone to a nearby shelter that helps support families by packaging food and giving away clothes. It's the only one in town where people in need can come get a grocery bag of clothing for free.

I went into their clothing department and started looking through. They had clothes for adult men and women, toddlers, little kids and ages maybe six to eleven, but nothing for girls entering high school. I know that's such a hard time, and I thought, "I could help out here." So, I went shopping and bought cute stuff in reasonable price ranges and donated them to the local food and clothing shelf.

The people at the shelter sent me a letter telling me a girl from the hurricane, Katrina, had come up to Minnesota to live with relatives, with nothing. She came in and had gotten some of the clothes that I had brought. She was very thankful that someone had thought of her without even knowing her. That was nice to hear. I was proud of myself. It just felt really good that I could help someone.

I guess I wish my parents would understand that I'm a teenager, now. I think I should be able to have more freedom even though they do give me a lot of freedom, I guess. I just feel like sometimes they punish me for things that are somewhat small.

I am most proud of my dad because he lost a lot of weight since my Bat Mitzvah. Over the summer, while I was gone he started working out. I am very proud because he wanted to do something that he wasn't forced to do and he accomplished it.

I guess I'd want to tell kids going through this shift that really, you are not different if you are from a divorced household. You're the same in every way, it's just your parents are living in two different homes and that's about it. We are just normal kids that you don't need to look at any differently. I know I'm lucky that my parents don't hate each other. I wish all kids could have that, and I do know a lot of them at my school, who have it sort of the same, but I know a lot who have it very different, too.

What pleases me most about my parents no longer being married is that they both have different rules. They don't have different rules, but, like my mom is a little bit more strict about my homework always being done, and even though when I'm at my dad's, like he is not as strict, it always gets done, though, it maybe takes a little longer than it would at my mom's. And I like that I have two rooms and I can decorate them both in anyway that I want.

Something that I have learned from my mom is that doing stuff last minute isn't very good, so I'm working on being on top of my homework without her nagging me about it. The most proud that I am of my mother is that she is actually promoting and publishing a book, and a website and movies! My dad showed me what work he does. Learning stuff like that, I really want to be in business, but maybe more in the fashion industry.

I really don't remember how it was when my parents were married because…, I don't know, we've always been together, I guess.

We're a family.

The Horrible Word Called Divorce

… My parents were the bestest friends ever by the end of the divorce. We still go on vacations together, it's way better than I thought it would be when they first told me about it!

This whole divorce had changed my life forever. It helped me find out that life can never be perfect; it can just be great with a few bumps in the road on the way.

The yelling, the screaming has all disappeared, while the word 'divorce' is no longer a fear!

The End

CHAPTER 9 DISCUSSION
Recognizing Our True Nature

How much endurance or sacrifice is the determining factor in how great a love is measured? Why do we feel the need to measure love at all? How often is the sentence, "*I gave up everything for you*" something that comes between a couple, or a partnership? *I do everything and get nothing in return... I make all the sacrifice... I've stayed here all these years.* Is that a testament to love? Being within a relationship that feels like a 'binding' of soul does what good for whom?

We also have relationships with ideas. The idea of marriage or divorce that has been imprinted on humanity for millennia is changing, as is all else in our worlds. We may have a relationship with the idea of abandonment. Abandonment lives in the neighborhood of *Victim-hood*, *Betrayed-ville*, and *Blames-town*. We've all traveled through at least one of these in our lives. But what determines who stays and who leaves?

There is a term that I choose to use as a tool in my awareness of my life and purpose. Witnessing "synchronicity" in life, when the phone rings and it's the person we were just thinking of a moment ago, or when you know there is something knocking on the door of your awareness, making you wonder if there is some coincidence that some subject is coming at you from various sources. Coincidences are more than just that, they are the moments in life where we choose to attune to our guides, or not. Are we awake or asleep, do we notice or ignore those moments in our life?

In certain traditions of Numerology, or the study of numbers and their divinatory meaning, it is interesting that this 9th chapter deals with integrity, as does the number 9 in my favorite numerology book. When integrity is an issue in our life, we have the opportunity to witness it from every latitude and longitude, from within its definition and from outside of it.

Integrity means that our thoughts, words and actions support one another.

Our words express our thoughts and they are expressed in our actions. One can say one thing yet do another, and then have to recognize that they didn't have integrity. It isn't a quality that we grow up just having, it needs to be cultivated. A child must learn the difference between what they say and what they do.

When we have cultivated integrity, then we needn't question ourselves on what is right or wrong to do. Sometimes, what seems 'wrong' is exactly what is 'right' for that situation. If you can observe the synchronous events, gain perspective each time another one happens, and recognize that your perspective will be different on the next round (and the next round...,) then living with 'the flow' becomes an exciting adventure in life.

Synchronicity requires spontaneity to follow through, because it often shows up when we have made other plans. But that is precisely the point; those moments are little nudges that show us another avenue. It might still have potholes in which to fall, but there is some reason it was brought to awareness. We may not find out the reason why for many years. That is where faith comes in. Not blind faith, but faith built upon experiences when we did listen to those hunches, and when we did not. Those experiences give us the basis to trust our 'gut.'

Trusting our own voice in the head comes down to listening if it is truly our own voice, or one we have accumulated through socialization. The voices that shout "You can't do that!" are usually from someone else in our life telling us not to shine. We may not even remember that conversation, but it left an imprint that if you want to be accepted than you must follow certain rules... When your inner voice tells you to break those rules, what is the basis of emotion underlying it? How does the body feel when thinking about it? Are we raging with fury in making that decision, or does it feel calm, even if scary. Is the motivation pure? And just who defines pure? The Puritans?

Having integrity to self requires learning what is 'pure' to us as individuals. If my body is hungry, thirsty or tired, those are pure sensations. Just as giving someone a kiss spontaneously is pure feeling in action, whatever the rules society places on that deed. Our experiences and true nature dictate the purity of that spontaneous kiss. What a kiss means to one may mean something entirely different to another. Yet, there are so many types of kisses: one for a child or parent, another for a lover, and still another for a reverence to someone or thing. These are just examples. It could be about cleaning the house... how one does something comes from their experiences combined with their true nature. When experiences overrule someone's true nature, there is conflict in the mind about what has integrity. What we are taught about love, versus how we feel about love may be two conflicting aspects that continuously butt heads between our mind and our heart.

We are taught that fury and rage are 'bad.' Conversely, we learn "What feels right is what is right," unless it is untamed fury, *but even that has its necessity.* The fury of a forest fire is absolutely needed to burn down what keeps the fledgling seeds from receiving light. Only the heat raised to the level of a raging forest fire will open those new seeds. It is the natural cycle, and when Forest Fighters tried to stop the process, they learned they were killing the forests by stopping the fires. So denying fury or rage from our being, when it is a natural seed within each and every one of us, is an idea that seems 'good' on a surface level, but perhaps may not be 'right.'

Many say, "My anger has nothing to do with fear when I'm angry about an injustice." An injustice, though, is an opinion based on one's experience. An injustice comes down to, in my opinion, an absence of compassion and absence of love, because *compassion is love.* Injustices come back to us through Karma, whether it is to our self or someone else. On the one hand, it may be considered an injustice to keep a child indoors practicing their instrument on a lovely day, or on the other hand, is it an injustice to not teach the child discipline enough to finish something, even on a lovely day? These are both very valid values. *Balance is the key.*

Balance is another concept taught through Yoga. It is not just about being able to do some incredible feat on two hands, but more about taking that practice 'off the mat' and into life. When balancing 'on the mat,' we must watch our breath as well as our concentration, for when they are disturbed, so is our balance. How we go into, maintain and come out of a pose can be seen in our relationships. Maintaining balance requires constant subtle adjustments, taking it a little farther, deeper or longer until we release the pose, or fall out of it. Is falling failure? Nope, just practicing.

Life is all practice.

Evocations:

1. Do I hold onto things longer than necessary? If I can consciously be aware of it, can I address it? Have I prepared myself for change?
2. Do I validate others? Am I "awake" enough to witness the goodness that surrounds me?
3. What do I do to keep balanced? How do I know when I'm off balance? What do I do when I fall, or fail?
4. What voices have I collected in my life, the 'invisible they' who whisper our fears to us? Where did they come from and are they still useful?
5. What conflicts do I possess within my *true nature* that are not acceptable? Do I hide them? Do I brashly throw them in the other's face?
6. If life is school that we are consciously attending, what classes do we choose, and which are mandatory? Do we follow a prescribed program, or make one of our own designs? Do we take classes that will challenge us or ones we'll glide through? Or, perhaps, a combination?
7. What type of vibrations do I want to resonate out into the world? What is my definition of pure?

EPILOGUE
Living Awake in the Dream...

Lee and I were recently visiting my Tanta (95-yr-old auntie) and found ourselves recalling about when the time had come to tell our family members about the divorce.

Tanta: It was most unusual and dear of the three of you to come together as a family. The way you said it, '*We have something sad to tell you...*' I immediately figured cancer. I thought it was a very happy marriage. It never entered our minds that you were considering divorce. I remember I burst into tears. Tasha put her arms around me and patted my back, soothing me, and told me not to cry. How old was she then?

Lee: She was almost eight. You're right. Generally, when people get divorced, they don't come together to tell the people they love what is happening.

Tanta: No, they don't.

Lee: How long were you married?

Tanta: Almost 60 years, just a week short of 60 years.

Lee: Did you ever once think...

Tanta: Never. I'm sure there may have been reason, but you didn't think that way back then. Many people my age say you just worked at it, made up your mind that nobody should know and we'll straighten it out on our own...

Lee: Interesting...

Tanta: Maybe it was good and maybe it wasn't, but for me it was, thank goodness.

Our visit with Tanta propelled a continued conversation between us during the car ride home.

Lee: Her response, "You didn't think about those things, never discussed them, you shoo those things away." They just didn't talk about any of their problems? Who knows what goes on behind closed doors...?

Julie: *And always acted like nothing was wrong, so everyone would think you had such a great life. A lot of that era was about how things looked on the outside, but there was such turmoil going on inside… that's why our generation has done so much therapy! Cuz no one talked about anything!*

Lee: Similar to when we were watching "Valley of the Dolls" with friends and I really wanted to just like it for you, the same that you wanted to sit with me and friends in the front row of a wrestling match and be 'gung-ho'… We did get married, but we didn't really become part of each other's lives. We loved each other, enjoyed each other, but when looking back on our marriage, there are things we did not compromise about ourselves and who we wanted to be. That was another reason of our moving on.

Julie: *So, I want you to say, very honestly, what I could have done to compromise better?*

Lee: Well, with what my thoughts were about marriage, the woman standing in the background of a man, you could have been more, you know, more barefoot, pregnant and in the kitchen. But, that is not who you were, basically. You wanted to have a life. You wanted to be out there and put your mark on the world. After a while, I understood that you weren't going to be that 'typical' type of a wife that, in my mind, is out there. I can look at it and say it's what the world is becoming as men and women become more equal. It's not just you.

What was your perception of marriage?

Julie: *I was sure that we were going to be different than what I had seen. I thought you knew I wasn't that barefoot, in the kitchen girl. I thought that's what you loved about me, found different, and exciting. I thought you wanted to spend your life with someone like that. I guess it kind of came down to "oh, sure, that's cute…" I guess your patronizing and "allowing" me to do what I wanted to do, you never recognized that I was never really going to "grow up one day and be the wife" you expected me to become or who you thought I was supposed to be. That was always very sad to me. It wasn't me that you fell in love with; it was the idea of who you wanted me to be.*

Lee: I think I was in love with you.

Julie: *But you didn't want me, the person I truly was, to be in your life.*

Lee: But you were…

Julie: *You wanted a wife, the kind you knew from your own culture and history, but times are different.*

Lee: You have an answer for everything.

Julie: *And, they are always correct! (Ha-ha)*

Lee: Who says you want to get married?

Julie: *I think that…*

Lee: Oh, I've already seen, I've only been married twice.

Julie: *What? What are you talking about?*

Lee: You were married to Oscar. That's me twice. I've seen the second marriage. I've lived the second marriage. I don't want to get married again, not to you and not to anybody else.

Julie: *You know many people said or thought that what I did with Oscar was all about being revengeful.*

Lee: That wasn't revenge. It was your escape. That was what you needed to be able to do to move on.

Julie: *Could you tell that at the time?*

Lee: No. Absolutely not.

Julie: *So, would you consider the possibility of being in a loving relationship if someone special does come around?*

Lee: How can I explain this? It's kind of like going to Nordstrom's and Macys, it's you know, Dayton's, Marshall Fields and then

Sears, I mean basically they are all selling clothes. One is selling it this way, and one is selling it that way. One's got this label, another has that label, but so far the end result is that it is just a piece of garment.

Julie: *Wow.*

Lee: Well it's true though, how many boys have you dated that you can't say something similar to?

Julie: *That they are garments?*

Lee: They are like different types of garments, but in reality they are all made out of cotton.

Julie: *There's plastic...*

Lee: Okay then, there are some that are synthetic, or what do you call that shiny fake stuff, nylon? No.

Julie: *Latex? Rayon? Yes, there are some artificial women, and men, out there!*

Lee: Whatever. I'm not saying that women are all garments; I'm just saying that they're like clothes. I have never found a shirt that I can't live without. It's just a piece of cloth. There is a shirt I just love, but you know, there are other shirts that are going to come by that I'm probably going to like even more.

Julie: *But, the shirts don't love you back.*

Lee: Sure they do, they make you feel real, real good. A nice cotton Mikael Kors shirt, my God! And you know what? I think I have a better idea today about what 'love' is versus what 'true love' really is and I don't think that anybody that I have dated really has a clue to what I mean by that. They might want to be with somebody, they might want to be a companion to somebody, and they might want to be taken care of. They might, you know, want to be seen, I don't know...

Julie: *I thought I was jaded.*

Lee: I don't think I'm jaded.

Julie: *Well, I'm just saying, to compare a relationship with a woman to a shirt...*

Lee: And I'm not comparing any of those people to you.

Julie: *No, I'm just compared to clothing. That makes me feel much better.*

Lee: I'm using it as a very simple analogy yes, but it is, in my opinion, a very true analogy.

Julie: *Well, I do agree that relationships come and go in our life.*

Lee: Okay, wonderful. So do you waste time in trying to make something happen? When do you know it is not going to happen? Julie, you should have a better idea today, than you did when we were dating, when we married, when we were divorced, when you were re-married. You should have a pretty good idea of what is going to work and what is not.

Julie: *I think it is easier to recognize it sooner but it doesn't mean that it's not worth being open to.*

Lee: Oh, no doubt about it, but there hasn't been anybody that has been worth opening up to, or waiting for that thing to open, it's just not there and that's okay. I'm not disappointed. I don't feel jaded at all. I feel more, I don't know...sometimes I feel like I've been given a second chance in my life when we divorced. It's weird, but it's true.

Julie: *Second chance at what?*

Lee: At being able to love myself more, find out more about myself and being more for me first. I really don't compromise myself today as much as I used to. I don't fall into traps about what people expect, where I once did. I really don't. One of my greatest fears about getting divorced was about what would people say. Well, you know what do people say now? They say more about me now than before and I really don't care. I really don't care. We are doing this to reduce the percentage of people who divorce, not to increase it. That's why we are doing this.

Julie: *Yes, whatever marriage that can be saved is wonderful, as long as there is growth allowed for each individual. You've even admitted to how much more you like yourself now. I think we are speaking to people that are considering getting married, as well as those who are already married and considering divorce, right?*

Lee: Correct.

Julie: *I don't know if I'll ever be married again to anyone other than myself, even though I'm happy to have relationships.*

Lee: I think we're doing pretty well.

Julie: *I think we do still love and honor each other...*

Lee: Oh, definitely. We're there for each other in sickness and in health. We're there for each other in good times and bad times, poor and wealthy times. Our vows, if you really think about it, we've basically stuck to what we said underneath that holy enshrinement of the chuppah. We will be there for each other till death do us part. I do believe that.

Julie: *There is that whole line about forsaking others that hasn't been kept.*

Lee: What does that mean?

Julie: *It's not being with anyone else.*

Lee: Oh.

Julie: *Right. Yeah, that particular vow.*

Lee: Well, one out of seven ain't bad. C'mon. We're not perfect. We're human. It's ok.

Julie: *You're saying you think we kept all of our other vows?*

Lee: Well, most of them, we kept the ones that have the deepest meaning to them.

Julie: *Ok, but in marriages today, infidelity is a major reason why people get divorced, so what about the vow 'forsaking all others?' How does monogamy play into today's modern marriages? Obviously, if Viagra and Cialis are the two highest selling prescriptions on the market, there are problems all over the place out there. This is not just our own little problem; it's a generational thing... what gives?*

Lee: That vow was for the women. Men didn't have to keep it, and for many years, even in the Old Testament, men had several wives. But wives were meant only for their one man. Why do you think back in the day only men gave women a ring to put on their finger? It was because women didn't want to wear it around their neck, like cows.

Julie: *What page of your book is that on?*

Lee: Well, if you think about it, what is a ring? A ring is like a collar except it's wrapped around the finger.

Julie: *That's really funny, but a little scary, too.*

Lee: Men, the herders and the farmers, came up with it. They possessed bulls to husband all the cows (who wore bells on their neck or were branded somehow,) just like they possessed their women. They might have a favorite wife, but if they wanted another, they got one. Just give her a ring.

Julie: *So, the 'familiar story' goes like this: You get married, and live happily ever after. No matter what struggles you had to go through, the end reward is that you got married and 'lived happily ever after.'*

Lee: I don't remember any kind of story saying that. Snow White? Did she get married and live happily ever after?

Julie: *Snow White, Cinderella, Rapunzel... Shrek...*

Lee: I suppose you're right. Here's a great thing for us:
          They got divorced, and lived... happily ever after...

In Loving Memory of Oscar

The wind swelled, tipping the boat to a dizzying angle as the sails filled with the warm, salt-air. The "Jewel" triumphantly skipped across the shimmering depths with her captain-for-the-moment, Jules. She was listening to the wind, as he had taught her—to capture the essence of the song it was singing, depending on the tilt of the ear, or the boat. It was the most exhilarating moment of her life, terrifying as she faced her fears in the unfathomable depths of her liquid mind. She knew she would never hear the multitude of songs in the wind again without immediately coming back to this moment in time, and to loving him. She tasted the salt, as the wind whipped her hair across her face, slapping her vision back to the fears. They smell of demons, teasing and taunting, whispering in the wind what lurks under the deep dark… "Who will find you? You will be lost forever…" she hears as the tears cake down the sides of her cheeks. She grasps hold of the rich, smooth, worn wood of the helm with no one, nothing in site beyond the awe-inspiring 180 degrees of horizon. The captain holds her breath, tasting the ocean air. She realizes she has never been on the water like this before, except for in dreams.

Many blessings and thank you for joining us on our journey.

May the steps you take, raise your vibration…
May you resonate with goodness…
May your journeys be filled with life, love, overcoming fears,
and balance.
Bless your garden that continuously grows…
Cherish your surroundings…
Be patient with yourself and others…
Have empathy…
Be more loving…
Choose to have a better understanding of life…
Let bitterness be purified from the heart…
You are unique in everyway…

OWN IT! BE IT!! LIVE IT!!

Insight is forever changing…
Strive to never let the soil dry…
Sprinkle it with love…
For you, and you…

and YOU!

<u>Offer to impart that which you have to others.</u>

OFFER -- <u>to give without force…</u>
> In as much as we believe our beliefs, there is a potential tendency to need others to uphold our beliefs. To offer is to invite to partake of (physically, mentally, emotionally and/or spiritually), without force or provocation, whether for exchange or not.

TO IMPART -- <u>giving not everything we have, but parts to share…</u>
> To give a piece/percentage. Allowing those partaking to decide how much is comfortable for them to incorporate as their own.

THAT WHICH YOU HAVE -- <u>and only what is yours to give…</u>
> Love, time, self, care, knowledge, understanding, acceptance, compassion, blessings, possessions, and anything that would benefit them in a positive way. Release the fears, anger, hatred, judgments, possession, curses, and anything that would hurt their nature to be recycled into nourishment rather than toxic waste.

TO OTHERS -- <u>a person, situation or thing different than self…</u>
> People, animals, earth, universe, and your higher Spirit… those we know or don't know, love or don't love, need or don't need… they could be you at some future karmic point!

Made in the USA